BRAINLESS

BRAIN

The
Lies
and
Lunacy
of
Ann
Coulter

ESS

JOE MAGUIRE

wm WILLIAM MORROW   *An Imprint of* HarperCollins*Publishers*

HarperCollins books may be purchased for educational, business, or sales promotional use. For information please write: Special Markets Department, HarperCollins Publishers, 10 East 53rd Street, New York, NY 10022.

FIRST EDITION

Designed by Betty Lew

Library of Congress Cataloging-in-Publication Data has been applied for.

ISBN-13: 978-0-06-124350-9
ISBN-10: 0-06-124350-7

06 07 08 09 10 ❖/RRD 10 9 8 7 6 5 4 3 2 1

To my parents

The truth is rarely pure, and never simple.

—OSCAR WILDE

Contents

Contents

Contents

BRAINLESS

Chapter

Why Ann Coulter Must Be Stopped
OR
"Annoyance" Starts with "Ann"

> *Arguments by demonization,*
> *rather than truth and light,*
> *can be presumed to be fraudulent.*
> —ANN COULTER

You are (check as many of the following boxes as apply):

- ❑ Black
- ❑ Hispanic
- ❑ Asian
- ❑ a Democrat
- ❑ Jewish
- ❑ Muslim
- ❑ Gay/Lesbian
- ❑ Open to learning something

If you meet one or more of the preceding criteria, read on. If, on the other hand, you're one of the tiny minority of Americans who is white, male, and a staunch conservative proud of his bigotry, feel free to close this book now. Put it back on the shelf and walk out of the store.

On second thought, even if you *didn't* check a box, this book is for you. In fact, it's especially for you. Abbie Hoffman aside, not many authors would ask you not to buy the book they've just written. And this is no different. At the risk of overstating the case, what you're about to read may change the way you look at the world. And even if it doesn't, it will certainly change the way you look at Ann Coulter, who—if she is to be believed—has the only worldview worth considering.

Chances are, of course, you checked a box. After all, fewer than 20 percent of us are white, male, and Republican. And far fewer than that are the kind to shell out twenty-eight bucks to read the sort of prejudiced bile contained in Ann Coulter's latest book, *Godless—the Church of Liberalism*. But there it is on the *New York Times* bestseller list, proving yet again that we are more interested in controversy and colorful comebacks than we are in intelligent discourse. More interested in *The Daily Show* than the daily paper.

There's no denying that the level of political debate in this country has sunk like the *Lusitania*. Beyond the incomprehensible shouting that is the bread and butter of cable news shows, "serious" news programs these days offer little more than the pitting of one peevish pundit against another. The "politics of personal destruction" has gone from clever catchphrase to viable election strategy. The smear campaign is par for the political course. And while, in the words of the *Boston Globe*, "this darkest of the dark arts is likely to continue,"[1] that doesn't mean we should let it happen without a fight. We should resist such a thing with every ounce of our political awareness. The day we have a president whose handlers are adept enough to make it seem as if *he* is the war hero is the day we should take a closer look at who is directing campaign traffic. The day we consider it okay to cut down opponents without offering anything of substance is the day we need to re-evaluate who it is we're listening to.

This is where Ann Coulter comes in.

Of the dozens of talking heads responsible for the increasing polarity of our politics, Ann Coulter may be the most maddening. Rather than suggest a solution, she is content to lay blame. Rather than generate a game plan, she will merely point a finger. And so this book is for those of you who want to understand the damage that people like Ann Coulter are doing to America.

I read *Godless*, Ann Coulter's most recent book, because I wanted to see what all the hubbub was about. I had heard the quotes about the 9/11 widows and figured it was just more of the same old psycho I'd seen on TV. You know—the one who starts every response with, "Well, the liberals are wrong because . . ." no matter what the topic is. The one who thinks a hair flip and an eye roll is a rebuttal. But as I got deeper into *Godless*, it became increasingly apparent that she's more than just shrill finger-pointing. The arguments she makes are misleading to the point of being outright lies. On top of that, they're often irrelevant and typically directed at people rather than positions.

Normally, in the face of such blather, I'd move on and try to find something a bit more reasonable. But it's hard to ignore someone who tosses around words like "harpies" and "raghead"—especially when that person has been so sanctimonious as to utter the above quote about personal attacks. Ann Coulter is absolutely right when she says that "arguments by demonization . . . can be presumed to be fraudulent."[2] Which kind of casts a shadow over . . . oh . . . *just about everything she's ever written.*

To Ann, having John Goodman play Linda Tripp on *Saturday Night Live* is just another sign that liberals aren't fighting fair. It "isn't humor, it's hatred. They aren't trying to be funny, they're trying to make their victims hurt."[3] Meanwhile, it's apparently the height of rational debate when she says of four widows of the 9/11 terrorist attacks that she's "never seen people enjoying their husbands' deaths so much."[4] To suggest that their husbands would soon divorce them because their "shelf life is dwindling" and they'd "better hurry up and appear in *Playboy*"[5] is satire so sophisticated it makes Jonathan Swift look like Adam Sandler.

Coulter often claims that some of her more outrageous statements are, in fact, meant to be funny. She told *Time* magazine that it's the inability of people to see the joke that is the problem. "What pisses me off," she said, "is when they don't get the punch line."[6] Bear in mind that this was in reference to her "joke" that God gave us the earth to "rape." Simply put, the day the distinction is lost between Swift's satiric suggestion that the Irish eat their babies and Ann's claiming our right to rape the planet is a sad one. It's the day nothing is funny anymore. "A Modest Proposal" is a classic exactly because the Irish *don't* eat their young . What makes the rape-the-planet reference so unfunny is that it has been a way of life for half the world's corporations since the dawn of the industrial revolution 250 years ago.

Still, maybe we should give Ann the benefit of the doubt. We don't all have the same sense of humor, after all. If she's looking for a laugh, let's take it at face value. As she told *Time*, "Most of what I say, I say to amuse myself and amuse my friends. I don't spend a lot of time thinking about anything beyond that."[7]

At the same time, this lack of cogitation may help explain her later statement on CNBC's *The Big Idea with Donnie Deutsch* on July 1, 2006. "I believe everything I say," she told the host, who had dared to suggest otherwise.

Either way, Ann Coulter contends that "there are substantive arguments contained in conservative name-calling."[8] This might explain why she feels it's okay to say that former president Jimmy Carter "is so often maligned for his stupidity, it tends to be forgotten that he is also self-righteous, vengeful, sneaky, and backstabbing."[9] After all, we're talking about the guy responsible for the Camp David Accords and the SALT II Treaty (an essential step toward the end of the Cold War), and who, after leaving office, won the Nobel Peace Prize. Clearly, calling Carter "sneaky" and "backstabbing" is a sign of substance.

Accusing him of treasonous behavior for his vocal opposition to the war in Iraq, however, crosses the line into absurdity. If Ann Coulter, a self-described expert on constitutional law, thinks that our most popular ex-president[10] should be put to death for crimes against the country, where does that leave the rest of us? Ann Coulter's calling for the head of Jimmy Carter is nothing more than sensationalistic sneering at a statesman the respect for whom spans the

globe. It is nothing more than the sort of opportunistic mudsling-
ing that is her stock-in-trade.

At the same time, Ann Coulter probably considers herself to be
a big fan of Carter, if only in contrast to her views on Bill Clinton.
She's got an awful lot to say about our forty-second president, especially given that conservatives in America "are the most tolerant
(and long-suffering) people in the world."[11] And that tolerance
really shows in things like the following:

> When Clinton first showed his fat, oleaginous mug to the
> nation, the Republicans screamed he was a draft-dodging,
> pot-smoking flimflam artist. . . . So the Democrats lied.
> Through their infernal politics of personal destruction, lib-
> erals stayed in the game for a few more years.[12]

What Ann Coulter doesn't seem to realize is that she owes pretty
much her whole career to Bill Clinton. After all, his presidency gave
her her first book, *High Crimes and Misdemeanors,* which she has
deftly parlayed into a career as a well-paid pundit. It has also afforded
her the opportunity to make highly pertinent points about his
impeachment. Naturally, what she has done with those opportunities is to squander them to make room for McDonald's jokes and
assertions that Clinton is a rapist. And these are the sorts of things
Ann dredges up to make points about liberals *now.*

Then again, at least there's a tenuous link between Clinton and
today's liberals. Bubba was undeniably the left's two-term golden
boy, and he remains an influential figure in the Democratic Party.
His wife may be on the verge of a presidential run, and he has

10 PEOPLE ANN HATES

1. President Bill Clinton

2. Senator Hillary Clinton

3–6. The "Jersey Girls" 9/11 widows

7. Comedian Al Franken

8. Actor George Clooney

9. *New York Times* columnist Maureen Dowd

10. Herself

forged a role as an elder statesman of his party. So, holding him up as all that is wrong with liberalism—if misguided—bears at least *some* significance. If only all of Ann's arguments were as up-to-date.

While 2002's *Slander—Liberal Lies About the American Right* took on conservatives' nemeses such as the *New York Times* and . . . well . . . that was pretty much it, her follow-up was little more than a paean to Joe McCarthy. More than a quarter of *Treason's* nearly three hundred pages refer to the senator—who, many of you probably didn't know, was apparently one of the most beloved figures in American history. Or so Ann Coulter is determined to convince us.

McCarthy died—as in … *died*—a half century ago. Bill Clinton was ten years old. *Times* columnist Maureen Dowd was five. Ann Coulter herself wouldn't be born for another four years. Or six. She tends to lie about that. But the point is, denying the existence of McCarthyism while simultaneously blaming liberals for it is about as meaningful as saying 9/11 was the firemen's fault.

To be fair, *Treason* does contain a generous helping of Reagan worship and an effort to rewrite the history of the U.S. effort in Vietnam—as suggested by the rather windy subtitle *Liberal Treachery from the Cold War to the War on Terrorism*. And it has been Ann Coulter's best seller so far, moving nearly 400,000 hardcover copies.[13] And so, after sales slipped for 2004's *How to Talk to a Liberal (If You Must)*, which was primarily a compilation of her syndicated newspaper columns, it's no surprise that she went back to basics for *Godless*.

———

As if to outdo the anachronisms in *Treason,* Ann goes prewar for her latest tome. And we're not talking before Bush 41's little fling in the Middle East. We're going years before the big one. Dubya Dubya Two. Rehashing the story of Julius and Ethel Rosenberg apparently won't do. Ann Coulter is going to take us all the way back to the first Red Scare and the root of all our current problems: Sacco and Vanzetti. Oh, that and the Scopes Monkey Trial.

If only that were a joke.

You see, Ann's typical MO is to take a piece of history and turn it into a sign that liberals have destroyed America. Which would be easy to dismiss if she just weren't so darn vituperative. And off the mark.

The fact is, Sacco and Vanzetti were convicted . . . and *put to death* . . . for the crimes they committed. It remains to be seen how liberals can be blamed for the conviction and execution of two murderers.

But that's what Ann Coulter would have you believe. In her mind, *everything* is the fault of liberals. And everything is personal. Instead of simply asserting that she feels the 9/11 widows are being used as political pawns, she has to call them "harpies." Instead of simply questioning Michael Dukakis's record, Ann has to refer to him as a "Greek midget." Instead of . . . well, you get the point.

But even the nastiness could be excused if the arguments themselves were well-constructed. Solid reasoning—with logical conclusions based on valid premises—can be respected regardless of the rancor that accompanies it. Because let's face it, a lot of today's political debate is infotainment at best and outright guilty pleasure at worst. The sedate Sunday-morning talk show isn't nearly as much fun to watch as Jon Stewart calling Tucker Carlson a "dick" on CNN's *Crossfire*.[14] Still, when political discourse devolves into false accusations and bald-faced lies, we should all worry. When treatises packed with misinformation, malicious characterizations, and misleading sources become bestsellers, it's time to rethink our approach. And that's where *Brainless* comes in.

———

Anyone with a laptop and a modem can find list after list of Ann Coulter's more venomous statements. And while much of that bile is also detailed here, the overriding aim of *Brainless* is to separate the wheat of Ann's arguments from the chaff of her hostility. Even in these days of political correctness gone wild, we are too often willing to let slide the sorts of comments Ann Coulter makes. And it's not that she doesn't have the right to say them—clearly, she does. And it's not simply that she's a scoundrel. After all, I'm not beyond a snide comment or two. This book is called *Brainless,* for Pete's sake. I've worked in enough newsrooms to know my way around a pernicious insult. The difference, though, is that much of the banter there can be backed up with accurate attribution. Pity the poor bastards who can't. Lambs to the slaughter. Trust me on that one.

It's probably fair to say that the impetus for this book was my inability to accept at face value what clearly demands closer inspection. But more than that, it was my concern that people such as Ann Coulter are destroying any chance we have to right the ship of political debate. And the ship is listing badly.

Still, it's not all one-sided. When days of watercooler chatter focus on whether or not President Bush wore a wire during a debate against John Kerry in 2004, we've clearly lost sight of what is important. But moreover, when our attention is awarded to an author whose bold new idea is that liberals are a societal scourge to be blamed for all of America's ills, isn't it time to call her on the carpet?

This project began with reading *Godless,* where chapter after chapter contains unsupported "facts," attribution that is sketchy at best, and hypocrisy of dizzying heights. All from one of the supposed leading minds of the neoconservative movement. Throughout *Brainless,* you'll be shown the fallacies in Ann's discourse, as well as her insidious and inaccurate linking of those people and entities she dislikes with completely unrelated sources of contempt. You'll be shown dozens of instances of Ann decrying the alleged mistreatment of conservatives at the hands of liberals, even as she does the same in reverse. Ann's most flawed arguments are broken down into their component parts, deconstructed to gauge their validity.

Part of the problem, of course, is that there's so much malice and misrepresentation that it's difficult to combat it all. Reading *Godless* is like reaching that level of Space Invaders where the aliens are descending so fast that you can't even be bothered to take a shot at the spaceships flying across the top. It's all you can do just to focus on and kill the most immediate threats.

In Ann's own words: "When arguments are premised on lies, there is no foundation for debate. You end up conceding half the lies simply to focus on the lies of Holocaust-denial proportions."[15] Never is that more true than reading through Ann's books. It's Lucy and Ethel at the chocolate factory. The conveyor belt of misinformation is on high speed, and no matter how many little lies you nab, a hundred more get through.

And, truth be told, Ann Coulter is a good writer. There's no doubt she has a sharp mind, and her prose can be by turns entertaining and impressive. In an age when cell-phone text messages and e-mail emoticons pass for high literature, Ann knows her way around a paragraph. Which is part of what makes her seem so knowledgeable and authoritative.

Even so, the *how* of Ann's deceit is the comparatively easy part.

Especially with someone as ubiquitous as she is. Read a few of her columns or watch a couple of her television appearances. It won't take long to find an example of Ann's rancor, prevarication, or hypocrisy. It's the *why* that gets tricky. But read enough of Ann Coulter's columns and books and it becomes clear that her goal is simple: to undermine those who subscribe to any position to the left of her own by misleading the public into believing that the conservative movement will save this country from the hedonistic, corrupt, immoral ways of the left.

At the same time, let's not forget we're talking about a person here. We've grown so accustomed to taking potshots at celebrities that it's easy to lose sight of the fact that they have lives outside of their public personae. We're all so willing to think of them as deserving of scorn—or at least having forfeited the right to being treated fairly—that it behooves us to step back and think about it every once in a while.

———

I'm no psychologist, so speculation in *Brainless* about Ann's state of mind is kept to a minimum. Rather, in seeking some insight into the kind of person she is and what might inform some of her more controversial opinions, I've offered what details I could about where she's from, who she knows and hangs out with, and some of the people she admires. And it should be noted that I tried to contact Ann. I was lucky enough to get her e-mail address and sent repeated requests for interviews. None of them were answered.

Calls to her Washington, D.C., publicist were similarly fruitless. In short, it became clear pretty early that Ann Coulter is a very private person. And for good reason, it seems. *Time* magazine reported last year that she has had a number of stalkers, and that ever since having pies thrown at her at the University of Arizona in 2004, she is accompanied by a bodyguard. In April of 2005, she told the magazine that she believes one of the stalkers will someday kill her.

Whether or not we agree with what Ann writes, it's her prerogative to do so. She has every right to her opinions and, short of outright libel, can say pretty much anything she wants about anyone she wants. And whether she would admit it or not, Ann is also welcome to respond to the "sobbing hysterical women"[16] she claims are being used as unassailable liberal patsies. In fact, that's pretty much what her latest book is—an attack on the very people she claims not to be able to attack.

Similarly, we could rightfully respond in kind. We won't, of course—that would just be mean. Calling Ann a "bitch" because she called the 9/11 widows "harpies" is just stooping to her level. It's rear-ending the car in front of you to spite the driver for cutting into your lane. In that light, *Brainless* should not be considered an attack on Ann Coulter the person. Rather, it is a full-frontal assault on her methods, her mischief, and her madness. Part of that, naturally, will be an effort to understand what makes Ann Coulter tick. What motivates her as a person is no doubt intertwined with what spurs her on as a pundit. In that light, *Brainless* is an attempt to look at all of Ann Coulter, from her childhood to her childishness, her upbringing to her upbraiding of those who stand in her way.

Chapter 2

Ann on Beauty, Race, and Culture
OR
The Pot Calls the Kettle the "New Black"

> *In general, wildly overpaid narcissists*
> *are the last people who should be commenting*
> *on subjects of any importance.*
> —ANN COULTER, *Treason*

> *There is maybe just the tiniest element*
> *of projection and compulsion in all this.*
> —ANN COULTER, *Slander*

Like everyone, Ann Coulter has a view on just about everything. She's rabidly anti-abortion, opposes embryonic-stem-cell research, and thinks the theory of evolution is wrong. She supports the war in Iraq, advocates racial profiling at airport security checkpoints, and wants high-school kids to be taught sexual abstinence. But those are all *issues*. Yes-or-no questions. *Do you or don't you?* And which side a person falls on regarding the issues can say a lot. But how someone deals with other people can be far more telling. And how that someone deals with people from different backgrounds, social circles, or economic levels can be even more so.

Ann Coulter's attacks on liberals know no bounds, running the gamut from teachers to the editorial board of the *New York Times*. She is a terrorist herself, preferring bombast to bombs but similarly uncaring about the collateral damage she causes. As long as she achieves her goal of destroying liberals.

It goes without saying that Ann has nothing but contempt for those on the other side of the political divide. Her comments about liberals are pretty clear. They're vile scum, she's a paragon of virtue. They're abortion-promoting hedonists, she's a true Christian. There wouldn't be much to talk about if it ended there. Lucky for us, Ann spreads her scorn far and wide. Let's see just how wide.

———

Ann Hart Coulter was born in New York to John and Nell Coulter in . . . well, let's just call it the early 1960s. Her father was a lawyer—a "union buster," as she once put it—while her mother stayed at home to take care of Ann and her two older brothers. While born in the Big Apple, Ann was reared in Connecticut, the gateway to New England and the state with the fifth-highest median household income,[1] where more than 85 percent of the population is white.[2]

A reference to the Ramones in her senior yearbook and attendance at a handful of Grateful Dead shows lend a hint of edginess to an otherwise presumably preppie high-school tenure. But let's be honest here—growing up the only daughter and youngest child of a Connecticut lawyer doesn't exactly lend itself to the appreciation or understanding of things like gangsta rap, the difficulties faced by inner-city teachers, or, frankly, anything you can't get at a Starbucks or Banana Republic. We don't really expect people like Ann Coulter to have a rapport with a kid from the Newark projects. Which is not to say that it *can't* happen. Plenty of upper-middle-class kids from Darien and Westport go on to do admirable philanthropic work, developing a true relationship with, and sympathy for, the less fortunate and downtrodden.

Ann ain't one of 'em.

In fact, in her mind, Ann apparently *is* one of the downtrodden. Where she comes from, it seems that being a bestselling writer, charging tens of thousands of dollars to deliver your particular brand of wisdom to neocon college kids, and making appearances on Leno doesn't mean you've made it. A Palm Beach home with residences in Washington, D.C., and Manhattan may not be the height of affluence in Ann's world, but it ain't bad from most people's perspectives. Which is why blanket statements calling liberals "snobs" (four times) and saying they "thrive on the attraction of snobbery"[3] seem a little rich coming from someone who grew up in suburban Connecticut and was in the fencing club at one of the best public high schools in the country. But what really takes the torte is going on to say that "(w)hile the rich," and there she's referring to liberals, "are insulated from the societal disintegration they promote, the rest of us . . ."

To repeat: ". . . the rest of us . . ."

". . . the rest of us are protected . . . by our abiding belief in God. That's why religious people drive liberals nuts. Bourgeois morality allows people to have happy lives without fantastic wealth."[4]

This might explain why Ann is content to stay in her happy little corner of the world, living in a modest house and giving the majority of her money to charity rather than engaging in unabashed political opportunism, maintaining homes up and down the Eastern Seaboard, and charging groups as much as $50,000[5] to hear her speak. Clearly, it's the liberals who have all the means in modern America. Which is why, according to Ann, the left can afford to be so smug.

At the same time, there must be a *few* rich Republicans. Maybe, like, in government or something.

It turns out there are. And, graciously, Ann points out that "Republican multimillionaires are . . . more likely to have earned their money than to have married it."[6] The numbered citation there is mine. But it should be noted that Ann provided her own "attribution" for that "fact" in *Slander*. At the risk of overstating the illusory nature of her citation, it is quite probably the least meaningful of all the 780 endnotes in *Slander*. And that's saying something. Especially since this one is more than 120 words long—thus rendering it too verbose to reprint here. Suffice it to say that it merely points out that Republican senator Bob Bennett of Utah was a successful businessman, while John Kerry married into a ketchup fortune. It's no more a statistic than pointing out that Dick Cheney's two drunken-driving convictions, compared to John Edwards's none, means that Republicans are infinitely more likely to get stewed and drive than Democrats are. And liberals have got the *Kennedys*, for Pete's sake.

Then again, there may be a reason Republicans are seen as affluent—and, naturally, desirous of keeping their pockets full. Like maybe the fact that they're the ones who keep promoting tax cuts that would benefit them. Not enough? Try a November 2005 study from Washington University in St. Louis that found that the perceived shift in voting patterns in recent elections toward rich Democrats and poor Republicans is an absolute myth. The study ("Rich State, Poor State, Red State, Blue State: What's the Matter with Connecticut?") shows that since 1952, "higher-income voters continue to support the Republicans in presidential elections." The seeming red-state/blue-state divide—and the perception that the coasts are populated by rich Democrats while Middle America is packed with NASCAR-loving lower-income Republicans—is the result of Republicans having "the support of the richer voters within any given state but ... more overall support in the poorer states." Simply put, income varies more within a state than it does between states, and while voting patterns are more likely to match income levels in poorer (red) states, that is not the case in richer (blue) states.[7]

Of course, should you ever point out that the rich are far more likely to be Republicans, there's probably a good chance Ann would rehash her own February 14, 2002, column. "When did a lack of money and accomplishment become a mark of virtue? Some rich people may be swine, but so are some poor people."[8]

Then again, maybe Ann sees wealth as immaterial, so to speak. It's not what you've been given, but what you do with it that counts After all, she attended public high school in Fairfield County's New Canaan, where—if there's any truth to the movie *The Ice Storm*, based on the novel by Rick Moody and taking place during the Nixon era—all the town's parents were pot-smoking, profligate pleasure seekers. It was at NCHS that she perfected her thrusts,

parries, and ripostes as a member of the fencing club. She graduated in 1980, receiving an education that was evidently thorough
enough to get her into an Ivy League university. As such, it's reasonable to expect that her view of government-funded education,
and those who provided it to her during her formative years, might
at least be somewhat favorable.

Whence, then, the view that public school teachers are simply
"disinformational facilitators"?[9] That's just a baseless insult—unless,
of course she means those who would teach intelligent design in
science classes if it weren't for the fact that cooler heads prevailed
in places like Dover, Pennsylvania.

Much of *Godless* is spent decrying the state of public education
in this country. But at the same time, Ann's statement about the
incompetence of educators comes quickly on the heels of her
granting that she's "sure there are a lot of wonderful, caring public
school teachers out there."[10]

Of course, maybe she's just referring to those in New Canaan,
where there were about twelve students per full-time equivalent
teacher in 2003–04, compared with the Connecticut average of
fourteen[11] (and an average of about fifteen for schools in the rather
poorer borough of Brooklyn, New York).[12] While that pretty much
guarantees that New Canaan kids score near the top of the national
scale in readin', 'riting, and 'rithmetic, it comes at a price.

According to *The Budgets of the Fairfield Public Schools,* published
in February of last year, the 2003–04 net current expenditure per
pupil in New Canaan was $12,813, ranking it second in the state.
About two-thirds of that went to salaries, giving it the highest per-
pupil salary in Southern Fairfield County. Which may help explain

Ann's annoyance at being "forced to listen to their incessant cater-wauling about how they [teachers] don't make enough money."[13] Meanwhile "teachers in the private sector earn about 60 percent less than public school teachers. And their students actually learn to read."[14]

Equally heartwarming are the tales of those who overcame the burden of public school education. Take the late Supreme Court justice Felix Frankfurter, for example. It seems he "went to public school on the Lower East Side of Manhattan. Undeterred by the large class size and trifling teacher salaries in his tenement neighborhood, he went on to graduate first in his class at Harvard Law School."[15] So much for the idea that public school kids can't read.

Still, it's hard to take Ann's example at face value given that she earlier vilifies Frankfurter—who helped found the American Civil Liberties Union before being appointed to the nation's High Court by Franklin Roosevelt—for his writing of a book purporting to exonerate Sacco and Vanzetti.[16] (Yes, Ann's latest book contains a four-page diatribe about how liberals should be punished for presuming the innocence of Nicola Sacco and Bartolomeo Vanzetti—who, it should be noted, were *convicted* of a murder that they committed . . . *in 1920*. But fear not, *Godless* soon takes a quantum leap forward to Willie Horton and 1988, which—if still completely irrelevant—is at least a date within the past twenty years.)

Still, let's give Ann the benefit of the doubt and say she actually does respect Frankfurter, perhaps for his promotion of judicial restraint, not "legislating from the bench," as the conservative catchphrase goes. At the same time, Frankfurter dared to go along with his fellow Supreme Court justices in 1954 in prohibiting the segregation of public schools in *Brown v. Board of Education*. What a dilemma.

Good thing for Ann that it's not race in education that most raises her hackles. It's—you guessed it—sex.

To sum up her point: public schools "have more sex scandals per year than Catholic priests—thirty times more."[17]

Not to be a stickler, but if there's any contention, any assertion, any look-up-your-own-synonym in *Godless* that screams out for attribution, it's that one. And even if it's true (though how would we know?) that there are thirty times as many incidents of sexual abuse in schools than there are in Catholic churches, the allegation is so out of context as to make it absurd. In addition to being eminently disputable, the assertion that a child is more likely to be sexually abused by a teacher than a priest says nothing about the prevalence of sexual abuse in schools. It's like saying the likelihood of being hit by a bus is far higher in Times Square than it is on the Appalachian Trail. It's true. It just doesn't mean much. After all, there are far more schoolkids in this country than there are school-age Catholics—which is to say, the age when sexual abuse at the hands of an authority figure is most likely. There are also a lot more teachers than there are priests. And children don't typically attend church unaccompanied, which means they're less vulnerable than they would be in school.

But we digress.

The point, ultimately, is that we've been fed a number that goes unattributed and, even if true, doesn't carry any meaning. All in an effort to lend legitimacy to a lament about teachers' pay. (For much more on this, see the chapter titled "Ann Has It Both Ways".)

A perhaps bigger problem, in Ann's mind, is that public school teachers "have absolute job security."[18] Which is just an outright lie. Sure, teachers can get tenure, which makes it difficult to fire them without good cause.

Or does it?

Since Ann made that assertion in *Godless,* Williamsburg (Brooklyn) Charter High School teacher Nicole Byrne Lau has been dismissed for handing out information about salaries in New York's traditional public schools and trying to organize her colleagues to get better pay.[19] Clearly, Ann doesn't know the meaning of the word "absolute," which doesn't quite jibe with her statement about liberals "tossing around terms they don't understand, like *absolute* and *moral*."[20] (Emphasis hers.) It seems a little hypocritical of her to make such an accusation. Of course, Ann did go to public school, so maybe that's her excuse.

Ann's views on education would probably be a lot clearer if she could reconcile what seems to be pride at having struggled so mightily at an underprivileged public high school in the wilds of Connecticut with her Ivy League guilt.

While maintaining that "a lot of people who went to Southwest Texas Junior College are shrewder than Yale graduates,"[21] Ann has also called Ivy League universities "America's madrasahs"[22] (the Arabic word for "learning center") because they dare admit students who might demonstrate, for example, to demand that universities divest from Israel. The First Amendment right to peaceable assembly be damned, apparently. Which is an interesting condemnation coming from someone who considers herself an expert in constitutional law and was a litigator for the Center for Individual Rights, a Washington, D.C., firm that purports to dedicate itself to the defense of individual rights "with particular emphasis on free speech."[23]

At the same time, Ann can throw all ninety-nine pounds of her elitist weight around when she needs to. Such an occasion arose when President Bush nominated Harriet Miers to be a Supreme Court justice.

Eight of the nine current justices on the panel attended law school at either Harvard (six of them) or Yale (two). [24] Poor Ms. Miers, it is painful to point out, "went to Southern Methodist University Law School, which is not ranked at all by the serious law school reports and ranked No. 52 by *U.S. News & World Report*," Ann wrote in her October 5, 2005, column, lambasting President Bush for choosing such a numbskull. [25]

"I know conservatives have been trained to hate people who went to elite universities, and generally that's a good rule of thumb," Ann wrote in her column. "But not when it comes to the Supreme Court."[26]

———

Either way, it's pretty clear that Ann's views about government-provided education—specifically with regard to sex—and what it says about American society are sociopolitically expedient, to say the least. For better or worse, Ann is riding the wave of Republican talking points. Which means, naturally, that she sees fit to disparage homosexuals. Naturally, given that Ann reportedly has close friends who are gay, it's never as straightforward as simple gay bashing. Ann prefers to hide behind oblique references and innuendo.

To Ann, discussing Supreme Court Justice Harry Blackmun's majority (repeat: majority) opinion in *Roe v. Wade*, for example, is "humiliating, like discussing the plot of a 'Will & Grace' episode."[27]

Now, we all know *Will & Grace* jumped the shark in 2002 when they added Harry Connick Jr. to the cast, and it's clear that conservatives aren't allowed to say they like a show that has—*gasp!*—gay people in it. But the fact remains that *Will & Grace* was the number two comedy on television from 2001–05, which would seem to make Ann completely out of touch with a huge swath of America. And given the numbers, it couldn't *possibly* be that only the people on the coasts were watching.

Granted, it's possible to be both popular and inane. Just look at sales of *The Da Vinci Code*. But if television is that bad, then Ann should do us all a favor and stop appearing on it. And, for Pete's sake, stop touting *The O'Reilly Factor* as the top-rated cable show. At any rate, to point out that Ann used *Will & Grace* in her example rather than, say, *Friends* or *Everybody Loves Raymond,* isn't reading too much into it. She's too good a writer for anything to be accidental.

———

In fact, much of what Ann writes shows her simultaneous fear of and fascination with the gay community. And it's finely phrased. In what is undoubtedly a brilliant piece of prose on page 15 of *Godless,* Ann reviles *Rolling Stone* writer Jeff Sharlet for interpreting a comment by Republican senator Sam Brownback as a slur against gays when he quoted a line from the Gospel of Matthew saying, "You shall know them by their fruits."[28] Now, whether or not Sharlet misinterpreted the comment, or just saw an opportunity to criticize a Republican senator with whom his magazine's editorial board disagrees, doesn't really matter. The point—which Ann completely misses—is that Brownback's comment shows a complete lack of sensitivity to how words can be loaded with unintended meaning. Or, one shudders to think, an all-too-acute sense of what such words can do. Maybe Ann is totally aware of how to sting the opposition in the guise of being misconstrued.

In telling the tale of *Brownback v. Sharlet,* Ann goes on to complain that "soon gay groups were demanding an apology from the senator. (All I can say to that is: how niggardly of them.)"[29]

Outweighing points for proficient punctuation is Ann's complete misuse of the word "niggardly," which means "stingy." Given her Ivy League education, it's probably not much of a stretch to say she knows full well what that word means—and, thus, has used it just to provoke a response. While "niggardly" has no etymological relationship to the word "nigger"—thus absolving her, by the merest technicality, of any wrongdoing—it sounds like it does, and so people refrain from using it to avoid offending those who *don't* know what it means. It's an exceptional piece of writing. It also happens to be race-baiting of the highest order.

Individual instances of language that is insensitive at best and revealingly scornful at worst may seem insignificant in isolation. But the sum of Ann's sniggering is unquestionably discriminatory.

Rather than admit she doesn't understand black people, Ann reverts to broadsides about their culture. In denouncing environmentalism, for example, Ann says that "[t]he various weeds and vermin liberals are always trying to save are no more distinguishable than individual styles of rap music."[30] Why not say "no more distinguishable than individual styles of multigrain bread at the Whole Foods market"? Or "individual styles of khaki pants at The Gap"? Arbitrarily dismissing what you don't understand (and what is undeniably a huge aspect of popular culture) just invites criticism. And, sure, most Connecticut-bred white women probably can't tell their Tupac from their tokus. But to wear such ignorance as a badge of honor smacks of haughtiness.

That said, at least Ann stays somewhat current when she denigrates hip-hop culture. The smart money says Ann has never seen the "Sucker Free" countdown on MTV2, but at least she makes reference to a recent chart topper in saying that liberals base their positions on the "belief that man is just another animal. (And not just Kanye West—they're talking about all men.)"[31]

At the same time, it's difficult to see how Ann's Kanye bashing is different from a third-grade boy's tugging on a girl's pigtails because he can't deal rationally with his prepubescent crush. Look, maybe Ann is among the world's approximately thirty-seven women who *don't* want to sleep with Kanye West. Either way, defending President Bush against a charge of racism by making thinly veiled racist statements might not be the best course of action for someone who wants to be taken seriously.

Attacking the person responsible for a comment or viewpoint— in this case, Kanye's assertion that George Bush "doesn't care for black people"[32]—instead of refuting the validity of the assertion is what is called an ad hominem fallacy. The term literally means "to the man," and it's used to describe the tearing down of a person rather than a position, which is a philosophical no-no. As noted skeptic and author Michael Shermer writes in *Why People Believe Weird Things*, "(c)alling someone an atheist, a communist, a child abuser, or a neo-Nazi"—or, in this case, an animal—"does not in any way disprove that person's statement."[33] This is not meant to argue one way or the other about the president's feelings about black people. It simply shows that the proper way to dispute Kanye West's assertion is to garner facts and evidence that show otherwise. Calling him an animal doesn't guarantee that he doesn't know what he's talking about.

———

In addition to making frequent ad hominem attacks, Ann seems rather fond of the unscrupulous sales tactic known as the old bait-and-switch. A prime example comes on page 15 of *Slander*. And this one is particularly nasty. Consider the following passage (the three following numbered citations are hers and have been left in for reasons that will soon be clear):

> After Supreme Court Justice Clarence Thomas wrote an opinion contrary to the *clearly* expressed position of the *New York Times* editorial page, the *Times* responded with an editorial on Thomas titled "The Youngest, Cruelest Justice." That was actually the headline on a lead editorial in the Newspaper of Record. Thomas is not engaged on the substance of his judicial philosophy. He is called a "colored lawn jockey for conservative white interests," "race traitor," "black snake" "chicken-and-biscuit-eating

Uncle Tom,"[39] "house Negro" and "handkerchief head," "Benedict Arnold"[40] and "Judas Iscariot."[41]

Wow. That's a lot of nasty stuff in that *Times* editorial. Or it would be, if the newspaper had actually printed any of it, aside from the comparatively mild "youngest, cruelest justice" part—which is certainly within the scope of editorial-page decorum.

You see, what Ann has done there is mention the *Times* piece in close proximity to a list of severe racial slurs, giving the reader the impression that it was the *Times* that printed these horrible things. What makes her paragraph "factual," by the merest technicality, is the segue sentence: "Thomas is not engaged on the substance of his judicial philosophy." But the segue is weak at best and intentionally misleading at worst, since even *that* makes it sound as if the *Times* has not done so.

Only readers who flipped to the back of *Slander* to read the citations in the above passage would realize that the really rude stuff comes from other places. Here are the endnotes in their entirety:

39. "Interview with Jocelyn Elders," *Playboy,* June 1995 and passim.

40. Joseph Lowery, at a Southern Christian Leadership Conference meeting, quoted in *The New Yorker,* May 6, 1996.

41. Ibid.

"And passim" means "in other places or works," by the way. "Ibid.," of course, means "second verse, same as the first." No, it's short for "ibidem," and it means "in the same chapter, page, etc." But even if you didn't know that, it now becomes clear that the *Times* is not responsible for the insulting language.

What Ann has done may be a brilliant way to impute the Gray Lady with such prejudice while retaining the Get Out of Jail Free card of technical accuracy. And there is no shortage of writers in this country, especially those of a political bent, who take advantage of such a skill. Effectively, that places the burden of understanding on the reader's shoulders. Journalists who care about clarity, on the other hand, subscribe to the idea that the reader should have to do as little work as possible. Making a point is one thing. Leading the reader up the garden path is downright sneaky.

But the sneakiness doesn't end there.

Ann's web of misdirection is so remarkably complex that even after uncovering the fact that the *Times* wasn't responsible for the litany of slurs, the reader is hardly closer to the truth than before. As pointed out by media watchdog the Daily Howler (www.dailyhowler.com), a check of the endnotes leaves the reader with the impression that former U.S. surgeon general Jocelyn Elders is guilty of using much of the offending language.

Not so.

"In fact, Coulter's faking went well beyond her bogus claims about the *Times*," the Howler wrote the week she appeared on the cover of *Time*. The endnotes "were thoroughly bogus too! No, those nasty phrases didn't come from Joycelyn Elders' *Playboy* interview. They came from a totally different source."[34]

The Howler points out that, just as the *Times* is innocent of the accusation that it spewed such racist invective, so is Elders. As is

Joseph Lowery, whom Ann mentions in endnotes numbers 40 and 41. Apparently, much of the nastiness comes from a "book review in the *Washington Times* . . . that has nothing to do with either Elders or Lowery . . . It concerned an obscure book on racial matters by Charles Lawrence and Mari Matsuda"[35] and contained the following passage (abbreviated with ellipses to cut to the chase):

> The violent implications of [Lawrence and Matsuda's] analysis are apparent from the hate-laden language criticizing . . . Supreme Court Justice Clarence Thomas. In over 75 references to Justice Thomas, the authors use images designed to evoke hatred: "race traitor," "black snake," "chicken-and-biscuit-eating Uncle Tom," "house Negro," and "handkerchief head."

While the implication from the *Slander* endnote cited *Playboy*'s interview with Elders, "none of those phrases came from that session."[36] In other words, that's a pretty huge "and passim." Like, enormous. According to the Howler, here is the former surgeon general's full exchange regarding Clarence Thomas:

PLAYBOY: What about Supreme Court Justice Clarence Thomas?

ELDERS: I think Clarence Thomas is an Uncle Tom.

Silence.

PLAYBOY: No more on that for us?

Elders remains silent.[37]

Okay, so Elders did call Thomas an Uncle Tom. Nasty, perhaps, but not quite as bilious as "chicken-and-biscuit-eating Uncle Tom," which may be why Ann felt the need to juice it up a little.

———————

Whether it's worse to fabricate citations or to simply make unattributed nasty assertions is a matter of some debate. Either way, it's pretty foul stuff. And Ann is guilty of both. Take her statement that during the 2000 presidential campaign, Al Gore "aggressively implied that Bush's Supreme Court nominees would bring back slavery."[38] Now assuming for even a nanosecond that such a thing is true, even the most devoted reader would probably like to know a little more detail about that. Like, maybe see an actual statement to that effect.

Oh, but wait—maybe there is one. Ann sets us up by saying that Gore's implication included that "Justices Antonin Scalia and Clarence Thomas were already hard at work on the Republicans' pro-slavery initiative."[39] She goes on to quote the then vice president as objecting to the potential appointment of "strict constructionists" to the court and how it reminded him of the "strictly constructionist meaning that was applied when the Constitution was written and how some people were considered three-fifths of a human being."[40] Ah, well—now we're to the heart of the matter. Gore, quoted directly from . . . well, we still don't know because there's *still no attribution*. There are only a few explanations for this conspicuous lack of a citation: 1) Ann intentionally left it out for some unknown reason; 2) Ann either forgot or was too lazy to add the citation; 3) Gore never said such a thing, and so there's no legitimate citation to make.

But we're not seeing the forest for the wooden speaker, here. Maybe Gore *did* say he objected to the appointment of strict constructionists to the Supreme Court. (He did, by the way.[41]). And maybe by doing so he *did* insinuate that strict constructionists are about as current-thinking as slave owners. But to call that an aggressive implication that Bush would appoint a court to reverse the Emancipation Proclamation is a leap of Evel Knievelian dimensions. It's simply absurd on its face. Was Gore baiting the opposition in one of the most hard-fought presidential campaigns in history? Probably. Was it dirty pool? Your call. Did he say Justices Scalia and Thomas wanted to bring back slavery? No.

———

Ann has a lot to say about race relations in this country. And in an effort to show how indiscriminating we are, she points out that "white murderers already receive more death sentences than black murderers."[42] Ann's footnote to this "fact" refers to a *New York Times* article that mentions that a Justice Department study conducted under presidents Clinton and George W. Bush showed that "U.S. attorneys sought the death penalty in 81 percent of the cases when the defendant was white, 79 percent when the defendant was black." On top of the fact that a two-percentage-point difference is what is known to sentient human beings as "statistically insignificant," there's a huge difference between a prosecutor's *seeking* the death penalty and a defendant's *getting* it.

Some numbers from Ann's home state of Connecticut contradict her assertion that capital punishment is meted out evenly. According to a March 2005 study done for the Connecticut General Assembly, of the almost 3,500 people on death row nationwide, 46% were white, while 42% were black. In other words, as the study says, "Race is a factor that influences the outcome of capital cases."[43]

Take a guess what "influences the outcome" means.

———

Meanwhile, Ann would have us believe that "since 1981, most serious crimes have declined dramatically in the United States."[44] How convenient that she should choose the start of the Reagan era as the kickoff for the drop in crime, given that University of Chicago economics professor Steven D. Levitt and *New York Times* writer Stephen J. Dubner make clear in their book *Freakonomics* that the truly significant decline began "in the early 1990s"[45] and that "homicide fell at a greater rate in the 1990s than any other sort of crime."[46]

Ann goes on to say—without any attribution at all, of course—that Clinton's "idiotic" program known as Community Oriented Policing Services (COPS) was "designed to spend more money on fax machines at rape crisis centers than on new cops."[47] Rather, she asserts that the crime rate "went down mostly because Republican legislature built a lot of prisons and because Rudy Giuliani was elected mayor of New York."[48] But Levitt and Dubner show that from 1990 to 1993—which is to say, the four years *before* Ann's beloved Saint Rudy took office—the "rate of property crime and violent crime, including homicides, had already fallen nearly 20 percent."[49]

———

Incidentally, Levitt and Dubner largely discount the role the booming Clinton economy played in reducing crime. (I just thought I'd take the opportunity to mention the "booming Clinton economy.") In any event, the authors make clear that the per capita murder rate in what is modern-day Italy, for example, has dropped from a heinous 56 per 100,000 people in the thirteenth and fourteenth centuries to just 1.5 per 100,000 for the period 1950–94.[50] No doubt Ann credits Pope Innocent III[51] for jump-starting the reduction in crime.

Whether or not you buy into Levitt and Dubner's argument that 1973's *Roe v. Wade* "help[ed] trigger, a generation, later, the greatest crime drop in recorded history"[52]—a compelling, if politically incorrect, theory—you can't argue that this precipitous drop occurred while Ann's pal Bill Clinton was in office.

———

Beyond her misunderstanding of crime trends, Ann is pretty out of touch with the common folk. Citing that liberal rag the *New York Times*, she writes that at Harvard University, "90 percent of the students come from families above the median income in America ($42,000 a year). Nearly 80 percent come from families in the top 20 percent ($80,000)."[53] Who in their right mind thinks that's a *good* statistic? How is socioeconomic homogeneity at Harvard—a citadel of higher learning, in the truest sense of the word—a valued condition? Unless you think the American Dream is actually conferred upon those who grew up white and privileged. And this comes from a woman who self-righteously wrote in her senior yearbook entry that she is "against the homogenizers in art, in politics, in every walk of life." Except, it seems, the walk of life that gets you into the country's elite universities.

While Ann's alma mater, Cornell, was the first of what would become the Ivies to allow women students, it has suffered its share of racial tension. In 1969, its president, James Perkins, resigned in the wake of student protests that saw members of the university's Afro-American Society arm themselves and take over the student union building during parents' weekend.[54]

But this is not to suggest that Ann prefers to sit in her ivory (-skinned) tower, beyond the reach of opponents' criticism. On the contrary, a self-described stirrer of the political pot, Ann gets a little testy when ignored. To someone with her sense of self-importance, being overlooked is a far worse fate than being challenged. Clearly, Ann is the type of person who thrives on intellectual confrontation. As we will explore further in the chapter that looks at Ann's misogyny ("Ann on Women"), she's also in need of the limelight. Which is probably why she gets a little whiny when the world occasionally turns the other cheek.

In a June 15, 2006, essay on her Web site, Ann complained that "no one has made a peep about that swipe I took at Hillary [Clinton], proposing that she have a chat with her husband before accusing others of being 'mean' to women in light of Juanita Broaddrick's charge that Bill Clinton raped her."

Here's hoping you're appeased, Ann.

Though, admittedly, it may not be enough until she is fully denounced by everyone in what she constantly refers to as the MSM—the mainstream media. "The establishment's current obsession with me is the MSM's last stand," she wrote. "They've deployed the whole lineup of yesterday's power brokers against me, and all they've accomplished is to make my book the No. 1 book in the country. In other words, their efforts to defeat me have just created more people like me."[55]

At the risk of getting all Freudian here, it's pretty clear that Ann has many of the characteristics of what is called "narcissistic personality disorder." It's a charge that, much to Ann's undoubted delight, has also been leveled at one of her primary antagonists—as detailed in the book *Michael Moore Is a Big Fat Stupid White Man* by David T. Hardy and Jason Clarke. In the book, the authors point to Moore's sense of entitlement, his arrogance, and his belief that others are envious of him.[56] Though it is primarily a condition seen among men, women suffer from it as well. And while it often can be a sort of case of arrested development (children, after all, are the world's biggest narcissists), a related condition known as "acquired situational narcissism" can set in later in life. Writing in the *New York Times Magazine* in December of 2001, Stephen Sherrill quotes Cornell Medical School psychiatry professor Robert B. Millman as saying that fame and money can not only distort a person's view of the world but push them over the edge into narcissistic personality disorder.[57]

Which may help to explain Ann's belief that she is a trendsetting style maven.

"Originally, I was the only female with long blonde hair," she told conservative Web site CapitolHillBlue.com in June of 2000.

"Now they all have long blonde hair." It's probably only a matter of time, then, until "they" all start wearing size-0 minidresses and jeweled crosses around their necks.

Whether or not there are a bunch of little towheaded Coulterian foals now running around is a matter of some debate, of course, of course. Either way, while Ann is, as she told *TV Guide* in August of 1997, "emboldened by [her] looks to say things Republican men wouldn't," such appearance-assigned authority doesn't extend to people who actually forge a livelihood from their attractiveness. "Through movies, magazines, and TV," Ann writes, "liberals promote a cult of idealized beauty that is so extreme as to be unimaginable. We must listen to Hollywood airheads like Julia Roberts and George Clooney because they are beautiful."[58]

To recap: because she has a decent hairstylist, Ann gets to say things other Republicans don't. On the other hand, being handsome disqualifies George Clooney from having a valid opinion. (Wild guess: Mel Gibson, by virtue of his being a conservative Catholic, somehow retains the right to speak.)

———

It doesn't take much digging to unearth Ann's hatred of Hollywood, actors, and musicians. To Ann, a "high IQ is generally an impediment to being a good actor."[59] Never mind that two-time Academy Award winner Jodie Foster graduated magna cum laude from Yale, Academy Award winner Matt Damon left Harvard just twelve credits short of graduation to pursue his acting career, and Brooke Shields is a Princeton grad.[60] The bottom line is, if you don't agree with Ann, you can't possibly be intelligent. On top of that, any signs you may show that you *are* intelligent become fodder for immediate ridicule.

In the case of Academy Award winner Dustin Hoffman (who, let's be fair here, dropped out of Santa Monica College after a year), it was his use of the word "hegemony" in talking about the reasons for the war in Iraq that set Ann off. "Hoffman refused comment when asked to spell 'hegemony,'" she jokes.[61]

But let's be frank. The Rain Man never had true leading-man looks to begin with. And now that he's getting on in years, it's hard to criticize him for being beautiful. Either way Ann has plenty of reserve rancor for those of artistic mien. In perhaps the most exquisite irony in the Coulterian oeuvre, maybe the most fabulously misguided statement in the annals of Anndom, she says, on page 246 of *Treason*, that in general "wildly overpaid narcissists are the last people who should be commenting on subjects of any importance."

———

But maybe all this is just another example of her simply "flit[ting] from one rightwing prejudice to another, taking not so much as a gasp for oxygen," as the U.K. newspaper the *Guardian* said in 2003. "In a couple of sentences, she can play with overt racism, soften it with a line so provocative she could only be kidding, then round off the performance with a sweeping smear of the liberal enemy. Coulter has turned riffs like that into an art form."[62]

Indeed she has; her barbs are nothing if not artistic. But she does occasionally overstep, going from critical to crass—vituperative to vulgar, if you will. And while some level of latent anti-Semitism may inform her opinion of Hollywood, she saves the outright obnoxiousness for other targets. Such as her comment—in an assertion that liberals don't understand the word "constitutional"—that "the following sentence makes sense to liberals: President Clinton saved the Constitution by repeatedly ejaculating on a fat Jewish girl in the Oval Office."[63]

Without defending presidential priapism, it makes sense to question what Monica Lewinsky's religious affiliation has to do with anything. Moreover, in what way does her shopping at Lane Bryant come into play? Similar to an ad hominem attack (and fallacy), this use of so-called emotive words ("fat," "Jewish") can be a hindrance to rational thought. As Shermer says in *Why People Believe Weird Things*, "(e)motive words are used to provoke emotion and sometimes obscure rationality."[64]

Compare the above to Ann's assailing of liberals for their alleged attacks on such women as Linda Tripp and Katherine Harris. "There is nothing so irredeemably cruel as an attack on a woman for her looks. Attacking a female for being ugly is a hideous thing, always inherently vicious."[65]

Well said.

But maybe Ann has hit on a solution: plastic surgery. Breast implants, in particular. While there is far more cleavage, not to mention far fewer wrinkles, on the cover of this year's *Godless* than can be seen on the cover of 2003's *Treason*, that may all be attributed to the magic of Adobe Photoshop.

In any event, more than a little of *Godless* is spent in an effort to debunk the view that silicone breast implants are dangerous. It's hard to say whether Ann is simply a big proponent of mammarian enhancement on an aesthetic level, or she took a bath on Dow Corning shares. Either way, citing a CBS News report by notorious horrible person Connie Chung from December 1990, Ann alleges that the science showing silicone breast implants to carry unforeseen side effects is inconclusive at best and imaginary at worst. She goes on to bemoan the Food and Drug Administration's banning of the implants in 1992, implying that then FDA Commissioner David Kessler had acted of his own accord, ignoring overwhelming evidence that silicone implants are safe, and did so merely to appease a few "hysterical" women.[66]

But here's the thing about the FDA: like it or not, there's just the teensiest perception, really just a hint of the view, that it gives too-quick approval to drug companies. That maybe it's a little too willing to take Big Pharma's word for it when it comes to drug trials. This is not to say it's true that the agency is a rubber stamp—but there is certainly that impression out there.

What is true, however, is that the FDA doesn't like to backtrack and pull stuff off the market. None of us likes to admit when we're wrong, after all. Like the rest of us, the agency does occasionally offer a mea culpa and ban a drug, medical device, or, in the case of silicone breast implants, a cosmetic. But it's not as if they do it willy-nilly. It's one thing to rail against the sorts of lawsuits that bankrupted Dow Corning, but it's quite another to allege that the illnesses suffered by women who had implants are somehow phony. In fact, the FDA has published on its Web site (www.fda.gov) a brochure detailing the complications that the implants can cause. Independent of that, and highlighted in the brochure, is a review by the Institute of Medicine, which found that just the *local* complications from the implants can accumulate and have not yet been well studied, not to mention being "the primary safety issue because they are frequent enough to be a concern."

Among those complications are galactorrhea (spontaneous lactation unrelated to nursing), hematoma (internal bleeding), and chest-wall deformity (gruesomely self-explanatory). Oh, and toxic shock syndrome—which, while rare, *can be fatal*. In other words, stuff just slightly more dire than the fatigue and flulike symptoms Ann seems to think are the only real problems. And if you think it can't happen to you, try this list from the brochure:

- Breast implants will not last a lifetime.
- Either because of rupture or other complications, you will probably need to have the implants removed.
- You are likely to need additional doctor visits, reoperations, or removals because of one or more complications over the course of your life.
- Many of the changes to your breast following implantation may be cosmetically undesirable and cannot be reversed.
- If you later choose to have your implants removed, you may experience unacceptable dimpling, puckering, wrinkling, breast tissue loss, or other undesirable cosmetic changes of the breasts.

So, Ann can call lawsuits against Dow Corning a "scam" if she likes, but to say there's no scientific support for a link between breast implants and health problems is an outright lie. And seemingly inexplicable. Just why Ann so vehemently argues in (eighteen-hour) support of such a thing is a mystery that rivals her unquenchable thirst for the spotlight.

A lot of Ann's quest for attention comes from her feeling slighted by the media (perhaps not realizing that she's *in the media*), and her perception of a liberal bias at American news outlets. Never mind that "(i)n July 1995 . . . Jerry Brown was the liberal talk radio champion with forty-two stations. That same year, Pat Buchanan was on 170 stations, Oliver North on 122, and Rush Limbaugh was heard on well over 600 stations."[67]

Difficult to see the liberal bias there. But, okay—so conservatives have made inroads into the murky world of talk radio. It's book publishing that's the real problem—or so Ann would have you believe.

"Vast agglomerations of money are deployed to publish and promote liberal authors," she writes in *Slander,* and "[l]udicrous uncompensated advances are made to support liberal authors, and liberal jeremiads make it to print without the most cursory fact-checking."[68]

Crown Forum wouldn't say what Ann's advances for *Slander, Treason,* and *Godless* were. Lucky for us, then, that her good pal Matt Drudge would!

Saying *Treason* would mount "a fresh assault on the charts with an explosive defense of Joe McCarthy," everyone's favorite muckraker says Crown Forum "signed Coulter to a seven-figure advance for the sizzle book." Assuming he meant seven figures to the left of the decimal point, we're talking a million bucks or more. And that was three books ago. Even if she got the same for the ensuing two, we're looking at a cool three mil. That's a lot of size-nine Ferragamos.

But it's a safe assumption that the advances Ann received for *Slander* and *Godless* were even bigger. In fact, Drudge says she got "one of the largest advances paid to a conservative author" for her latest book. Which kinda makes Ann's whining that advances are "pure wealth transfers to liberal gabbers" and lamenting that "[f]eminist Naomi Wolf is regularly given mammoth advances, averaging half a million dollars apiece"[69] seem just a tad . . . oh, I don't know . . . disingenuous. Even with the help of a thesaurus, I'm not sure of the best adjective for a million-dollar advance if half that is "mammoth." *Woolly* mammoth, I guess.

Advances aside, let's take a look at how much Ann might rake in based on sales alone. Assuming she gets a standard deal (unlikely, given her past successes), Ann can expect royalties of about 15 percent of the price on hardcover sales. The following figures are taken from Nielsen BookScan, which is sort of the central clearinghouse for publishing sales data, as of the week ending July 9, 2006. (The royalty figures are rounded to the nearest dollar.)

BOOK	PRICE	SALES	ROYALTIES
Godless	$27.95	188,105	$788,630
How to Talk to a Liberal	$26.95	302,073	$1,221,130
Treason	$26.95	396,555	$1,603,074
Slander	$25.95	333,166	$1,296,849

Added up, that makes for more than $4.9 million on those four books alone. And we're talking just hardcover here. So the next time Ann Coulter tells you, as she does in *How to Talk to a Liberal*, that she's not rich,[70] ask her where the five mil went.

But, look, whether they make any money or not, let's just say that getting five books into print, with or without even the "most cursory fact-checking," is roughly five more than most writers—conservative or liberal—ever get. Half the journalists in the world are trying to get a book deal. It's no exaggeration to think that thousands of writing desks around the country are filled with thousands of unpublished manuscripts. Go to the nearest Starbucks at about two in the afternoon and glance around. There's probably a half-dozen people in there jabbing furiously at their laptops as they try to finish their books. Ann, meanwhile, throws together a bunch of previously published columns, adds a couple things that were initially deemed unworthy of print (for a reason?), and the next thing you know, *How to Talk to a Liberal* lands her a cool $1.2 million in royalties. If that doesn't make every struggling writer in this country throw up in his mouth just a little, nothing will.

Yes, it's been quite an uphill battle for Ann. And so it's perfectly reasonable for her to target "mainstream publishing houses," which would, she says, "prefer to ignore the free market entirely and publish only books with the hectoring anger of a *New York Times* editorial." She says that publishers "react to conservative authors like Linda Blair to holy water."[71]

Again, not to quibble, but both *Slander* and *Godless* were brought to print by Crown Publishers, a division of Random House, Inc. It's probably a fair guess to say you've heard of Random House, a huge publishing house with more than 10 imprints and a truly far-reaching international presence. If not, a little book of theirs called *The*

Da Vinci Code might ring a bell. Either way, it's no stretch of the term to call Random House "mainstream."

To be fair, Ann excoriates publishers indiscriminately. She mentions Random House by name on page 132 of *Slander,* ripping them for lavishing advances on writers such as Naomi Wolf and for allegedly losing money on books by such writers. Maybe that's because, as Ann says, "empirical evidence does not contradict the thesis that conservatives read and liberals don't."[72] Nice use of the double negation there to make the argument just slightly more valid—which is to say, still obviously an outright lie. Never mind that the *New York Times* (that liberal rag) sells more than a million copies a day, while the leader of our country boasts that he doesn't read newspapers. But we're talking books here. And Ann inarguably makes it to the *New York Times* bestseller list just about every time out. (By the way, so does Al Franken. So does Michael Moore. So does—heart be still—Maureen Dowd. Go on, Ann, maintain your position that liberals don't read.)

Either way, it may not matter who publishes Ann's books. Conservatives are crafty enough to sniff them out. Or are they?

Ann says that "potential readers have to find a bookstore where they can buy" such tomes because "bookstores refuse to stock them."[73]

Excuse me for slipping into the first person here, but I bought *Slander, Treason, How to Talk to a Liberal,* and *Godless* at a Barnes & Noble on Broadway in Manhattan. I had to hunt for, oh, about a minute and a half to find the first three. The latter, on the other hand, was fairly prominently displayed. No, wait—I don't want to soft-pedal this. The fact is, there was a huge—HUGE—stack of copies right in the center of the store's ground level. There is simply no way any potential readers could have missed it.

The plain truth is that bookstores exist to make money and will stock books based on demand. Whether written by liberals, conservatives, atheists, priests, hookers or housewives—it just doesn't matter. If Barnes & Noble can get twenty-five bucks over and over again for a book, it's gonna get prominent play. But in Ann's world, conservatives' books are condemned. Banished to the backs of shelves if not outright hidden by shop owners. The problem is, it's not really true. Sure, there's probably a liberal bookstore owner here or there who won't put Sean Hannity's *Deliver Us from Evil* on the front table, but the Christian Science Reading Room probably doesn't have more than a handful of Jenna Jameson's *How to Make Love Like a Porn Star* lying around either. Bottom line: Hannity, Bill O'Reilly, the Swift Boat Vets, and Dick Morris, just to name a few conservative authors, make the bestseller list because their books get national distribution and because big bookstores sell as many as they possibly can.

———

But back to the matter at hand. It's pretty clear that favorable reviews, prominent display in places such as Borders and Barnes & Noble, and a host of marketing events all contribute to the success of a book. Part of the publicity push is getting airtime on talk shows and play in major newspapers' book sections. Too bad for Ann that "[n]o conservative book will have a major rollout on the *Today* show, be excerpted in *Vanity Fair*, lead to an appearance on *Conan*, or merely be politely reviewed in the *New York Times*."[74]

Let's go down the list:

1. **Today show.** Check. Ann appeared on *Today* for a tête-à-tête with Matt Lauer on June 6, 2006. Whether or not the interview constituted a "major rollout" of *Godless,* it certainly dealt heavily with her latest book and the controversial statements in it about the 9/11 widows.

2. **Vanity Fair.** Check. Ann was the subject of an undeniably racy question-and-answer session for magazine's "Roundtable" in June 2006. Conducted by George Wayne, the interview covered Ann's sex life, her Christianity, and her hair colorist.[75] Granted, beyond a couple of snippets of quotes from *Godless,* it was hardly an excerpt of her book. At the same time, it's far more likely that buyers of *Vanity Fair* would have read the Q-and-A than a chapter of Ann's latest tome.

3. **Conan.** I'll go ya one better: Ann appeared on the more highly rated *The Tonight Show with Jay Leno* on June 14, 2006. Leno introduced Ann by saying: "Her latest book, *Godless—The Church of Liberalism,* has debuted at number one on the *New York Times* bestseller list." Which leads one to believe they might have talked a bit about the book.

4. *New York Times.* Check. While it may not qualify as a polite review, the *Times* did do a story about *Godless* just after its publication. Citing Ann's "rhetorical compulsion" to say

anything to sell a book, writer David Carr said of Ann that "no other author in American publishing is better at weaponizing words." Ann "plays to win and is happy to take hostages along the way." On top of that her "sincerity is beside the point as long as people keep taking the bait." [76]

And there you have it. Four-for-four on the very things Ann claimed will *never* happen for a conservative author. Four whiny laments about how difficult it is for her, followed by four of the biggest marketing opportunities in publishing. Ann Coulter has trouble finding ways to hawk her books the way George Clooney has trouble finding a date for Saturday night.

Still, books is books, while television is the alpha and omega of media. And despite Ann's "ubiquity on political talk shows," [77] she seems to think that it's all conservatives can do to nab a slot on the box. "Outside of Fox News, the 'from the right' seat on *Crossfire* is one of the rare paid positions available for conservatives on TV," she writes. [78] She's forgetting, of course, her friend Larry Kudlow, whose *Kudlow & Company* appears every weekday at 5 P.M. on financial-news network CNBC. But Ann has offered the usual qualifier to make her statement at least somewhat truer than it would have been—in this case referring to "paid positions."

Granted, Ann's "paychecks come solely from writing and giving speeches. She earns nothing from TV," according to *Time* magazine. [79] But let's not forget that she was on the air on cable station MSNBC's very first day. [80] In fact, it was there that she gained celebrity as a legal correspondent and pundit.

That said, MSNBC found Coulter "blunt, rude and just completely over the top," *Time* quoted former MSNBC producer Stephen Lewis as saying. The network fired Ann in February 1997 for saying, as the network covered a memorial service for Pamela Harriman, that the once U.S. ambassador to France was the type of woman who "used men to work their way up." Apparently missing such incisive insight, MSNBC did rehire Ann, but was forced to sack her again after eight months for insulting a Vietnam veteran on the air.[81] Reports of the incident are about as reliable as information that has gone through three or four rounds of the children's game telephone, but suffice it to say she wasn't very nice to the man.

HOT OR NOT?

A lot of what Ann does on television talk shows is toss her meticulously kempt mane. It's her signature move. Like Clinton with the thumb thing. And claiming to be the original blond pundit "emboldened by (her) looks to say things Republican men wouldn't," she's clearly willing to play up her looks.

But is she really that hot?

What better arbiter of Ann's attractiveness than MSNBC's Chris Matthews. Speaking on the June 9 edition of "Hardball," Matthews, sixty, put the question to thirty-seven-year-old mop-headed conservative Tucker Carlson, early-forties MSNBC personality Rita Cosby and Mike Barnicle, former *Boston Globe* columnist and MSNBC regular, who is in his early sixties.

MATTHEWS: Do you find her physically attractive, Tucker?

CARLSON: I'm not going to answer that because the answer—I don't want to hurt anybody's feelings. That's not the point.

COSBY: Don't ask me that question.

MATTHEWS: Mike, do you want to weigh in here as an older fellow? Do you find her to be a physically attractive woman?

BARNICLE: I'm too old to be doing that. I had enough fights in my life.

MATTHEWS: OK, Rita, do you find her to be a physically attractive woman?

COSBY: I'll throw it back at you, Chris—do you find her attractive?

MATTHEWS: You guys are all afraid to answer. No, I find her—I wouldn't put her—well, she doesn't pass the Chris Matthews test.

So that'd be *not* hot, then.

Nonetheless, the seeming ever-presence of people like George Will on Sunday-morning network shows contradicts Ann's implication that conservatives are underrepresented on television. After all, though Ann's feelings about Tucker Carlson run toward the tepid, the bow-tied one is unquestionably right-wing and has certainly had a paying job or two as a talking head. Then there's Bob Novak, who, in a fit of now-infamous pique, walked out of his (paying) job in the middle of the Judith Miller melee. But who can blame him? What with all the liberal slings and arrows one has to endure just to get on television. After all, as a conservative, you "will simultaneously be described as ugly—and accused of being on TV only because you're pretty."[82]

It's demoralizing, what a conservative has to go through to get airtime. No wonder Ann has never appeared on the *Today* show or sat with Jay Leno—you know, those shows on the liberal networks.

————

In that vein, let's break for a quick pop quiz.

True or false: The following statement is more likely to have been uttered by a "wildly overpaid narcissist" than a normal person: As a conservative, you "will simultaneously be described as ugly—and accused of being on TV only because you're pretty."

The answer is . . . well, it doesn't matter. Because, to Ann, there's always another obstacle to self-promotion on the small screen. In what is perhaps her finest bit of what the *Guardian* calls Ann's "nutty logic," she asserts that a good part of the assumed liberal bias in the American media is the result of Republicans' not having "the wealth to own their own media outlets."[83]

————

"Indeed, the whole liberal media thesis is built on a foundation so shaky it can ignore, to name but two, Conrad Black's empire and Rupert Murdoch's News Corp.," the *Guardian* points out. "The latter's unashamedly right-leaning Fox network is changing the face of U.S. TV news, while newspapers such as his *New York Post* are cheerleaders for the right."[84]

In Ann's mind, she is "one of the most unpublished writers in America."[85] Even back when she wrote that—in *How to Talk to a Liberal,* which was, it should be noted, *published*—it was patently absurd. Ann is about as unpublished as Colin Farrell is celibate. Okay, so maybe the marketing and sales staff at the conservative weekly *Human Events* looks at the circulation of *Tiger Beat* with a certain wistfulness, but Ann doesn't seem to realize that just because you've written something doesn't mean it deserves to make its way into print. By incessantly whining that it should, you run the risk of sounding like a slightly saner Ted Kaczinsky—without the beard and math degree, of course.

Late in *How to Talk to a Liberal,* Ann regales the reader with the tale of how even the ultraconservative *National Review* rejected one of her articles after commissioning the piece. As she tells it, Ann was fresh out of law school and asked to write a piece on "Feminist Legal Theory." It was 1991, and Ann was about thirty years old. Or twenty-eight. Or somewhere in that ballpark. By her own admission, she hadn't yet understood what a word limit was, and submitted what can only be kindly described as a first-person polemic about what she perceived as the ridiculousness of the feminist movement. When, as she tells it, editor John O'Sullivan requested that she restructure the article to actually address the topic she was asked to write about, Ann concluded that there was "obviously nothing to be done."[86] How dare the editor of a national magazine request that a twenty-eight- or thirty-year-old inexperienced writer rework an article so that it even remotely resembled not just a piece of actual journalism but what he apparently *asked for in the first place*. The nerve of that guy.

But the indignity doesn't end there—no, no. Years after her noble battle against the *Natty Rev,* Ann was evidently asked to write a piece for *Cigar Aficionado* about campaign-finance reform. Like all fair and balanced articles, she began her piece by stating what she would do.

No joke.

The first word of what she submitted is "I'm." The first word of the second paragraph is "I'm." After using a bunch of other words in between (basically to blast the *New York Times*), her last paragraph starts, oddly enough, with the word "I'm."[87] One wonders what the problem might have been. Maybe the following exercise will help clear things up:

Hypothetical situation: To earn beer money during his summer break, a college student applies for a job as a mason's assistant. He is hired based on the qualifications conferred upon him by his owning a pair of work boots. Minutes after showing up for his first day on the job, he starts flinging bricks from atop a scaffold, complaining that he doesn't like bricks. Thinks bricks are "for suckers." Claims, furthermore, that houses are a left-wing conspiracy and that poor, put-upon Republicans have to fight tooth and nail just to own them.

After braining a couple of passersby, he is asked to stop with the brick tossing. He refuses, is paid for a day's work, and asked not to return.

Question: Based on the above information, who is to blame for the student's firing?

 a) The student for being an imbecile
 b) The mason for realizing he hired a nutjob
 c) The institution of bricklaying
 d) The *New York Times*

The answer should be fairly a)pparent to you all. And yet somehow it's a personal affront when Ann has an article spiked by an editor because the piece isn't what he wanted. If you order the chicken and the waiter brings you salmon, do you eat it, pay the bill, and leave? No—you send it back and hope the waiter doesn't spit in your food when he brings you what you want. Similarly, if a writer submits a three-thousand-word misogynist rant when he asked for an article looking at legal theory, he's unlikely to run it in the space provided.

To expect otherwise is insane. But that's what Ann is constantly screaming from the rooftops. She has the nerve to claim she's being denied her right to speak because of the media's liberal bias, and yet she's being afforded a chance to do so through the very channels she claims are stifling her. It's clear that Ann Coulter is concerned with little else but self-promotion, and unfortunately for the level of political discourse in this country, she is a master at it.

Chapter 3

Ann on Women
OR
Mano-a-Mano with the Fairer Sex

Everyone loves a catfight.

—ANN COULTER in the *Guardian* (U.K.)

Some of Ann's most venomous attacks are those against women. Especially those her pal Rush Limbaugh refers to as feminazis. You know the type: working women with the unmitigated gall to want equal rights; cosmopolitan gals who enjoy a fulfilling sex life outside the confines of marriage; *suffragists*, for Pete's sake.

Would that that last one were a joke, but it's not. On an episode of *Politically Incorrect* in February of 2001, Ann told host Bill Maher that women should "be armed but should not vote. No, they all have to give up their vote." She went on to say that "[t]he problem with women voting—and your Communists will back me up on this—is that, you know, women have no capacity to understand how money is earned. They have a lot of ideas on how to spend it. And when they take these polls, it's always more money on education, more money on child care, more money on day care."

As if in an effort to prove her own point, Ann allegedly filed an inaccurate voter-registration form in Florida in June 2005 and knowingly voted in the wrong precinct—a felony in the Sunshine State! Election officials there are investigating the matter, and documents apparently indicate that Ann gave her real-estate agent's address (which was a few miles away in the same town) instead of her own.

Ann evidently tried to vote in the February 7 town council election in Bethesda-by-the-Sea, where she should have been voting based on her actual address. But reports say she left that precinct when a poll worker began to explain to her that her registration address prevented her from voting in that precinct. Ann then apparently cast her ballot at the precinct where she was registered—which was actually the wrong location for someone having her street address. If that's confusing, you can see why elections officials in March gave Coulter thirty days to explain the inaccuracy, the *Palm Beach Post* reported.

In any case, it's pretty clear that Ann is baffled by the ballot. Take her assertion that "Democrats haven't been able to get as much as 50 percent of the country to vote for them in any national election for the last twenty-five years."[1]

This statement is true only in so far as it is masterfully phrased. Certainly, no Democrat has had as much as "50 percent of the country" cast ballots for him or her—in the same way that no Republican has, either. Even setting aside that a large chunk of the U.S. population is under the age of eighteen and therefore ineligible to vote (making getting half of our citizenry all the more difficult), Americans have a deplorable record when it comes to elections. In

1984, for example, when "voters in 49 states chose Ronald Reagan"[2] over Democratic challenger Walter Mondale, there were almost 168 million Americans eligible to vote, according to figures from George Mason University. About 55 percent of them turned out for the presidential election. In order for Reagan to have garnered even half of the eligible *voters* (never mind half of Americans, as Ann says) he would have needed the support of about 84 million of the just under 92.7 million people who cast ballots. Even carrying forty-nine states ain't gonna get you there.

————

Of course, Reagan might have carried all fifty states in Ann's world, where women wouldn't be allowed to vote, anyway. In fact, one of the problems with the United States is that "women are not prevented from doing even things they should be."[3] This, evidently, does not include carving out a career as a lawyer, writer, paid speaker, and television pundit. At the same time, Ann reportedly would love to be a traditional American housewife if Mr. Right came along. (Apparently, her first three Mr. Rights weren't so.) According to the *Guardian*, Ann would quit her jobs "instantly," since work is her main focus only because she doesn't "have somebody supporting [her]."[4]

Then again, perhaps it's not her busy schedule that keeps her from nabbing a provider. Maybe it's that "[c]onservatives have a problem with women. For that matter, all men do."[5] It's a safe assumption, then, that since "all men" have a problem, it would be wasted breath to suggest she try someone a tad more progressive with regard to women's rights. After all, in Ann's mind, there's little distinction between Democrats and *Playboy* magazine—both of which, she says, merely seek "to liberate women to behave like pigs, have sex without consequences, prance about naked, and abort children."[6] On top of that, "querulous little feminists [have] stripped women of the sense that they can rely on the institution of marriage and gave men license to discard their wives. But at least women can choose to be pigs now, too!"[7] So much for finding a Democrat worthy of her husbandry.

Still, like Elle MacPherson at a comic-book convention, Ann would likely stand out in the land of liberal lasses. Or so she says. "I don't think I've ever encountered an attractive liberal woman in my entire life."[8] Except, of course, for Gwyneth Paltrow, who, Ann insinuates, is considered to be a believable spokesperson for the political left only by virtue of her being gorgeous.[9] Then there's always the aforementioned Julia Roberts. And . . . oh, this is just silly.

THE ANN COULTER DOLL

Lots of disturbing stuff can be found on the Internet. The good news is that most of it's free.

In this case, it'll set you back thirty-seven bucks.

At a foot tall and as skeletal as the woman it's modeled after, the Ann Coulter Doll is just one in a line of "America's Real Action Heroes" from a Web site called TalkingPresidents.com. Dressed in typical black jacket and skirt, the doll is fairly anatomically correct, with legs so skinny they make Lindsay Lohan look like a pre–Jenny

Craig Kirstie Alley. But this special edition figure isn't just for show. Like Barbie's fascist aunt after too much chardonnay, this gal is infectious with invective.

To hear Ann talk, just press the belly button. You can't miss it—it's definitely an out-y. The sayings are a collection of *Slander*'s greatest grumblings, including such hits as:

"At least when right-wingers rant there's a point."

"Why not go to war just for oil? We need oil."

"At the risk of giving away the ending, it's all liberals' fault."

And, everyone's favorite:

"Even Islamic terrorists don't hate America like liberals do. They don't have the energy. If they had that much energy, they'd have indoor plumbing by now."

Included, in these days of litigious frivolity, is a warning that the doll poses a choking hazard for kids—liberal or conservative—under three years of age. And though it doesn't say so on the box, it should be noted that the Ann Coulter Doll is also a gagging hazard for reasonable people of all ages.

Clearly, there are a lot of attractive liberal women in the world, just as there are attractive conservative women. The above is just another of Ann's attempts to be funny or provocative or both. It's certainly not the first, which by definition rules out the last. And whether it's provocative is a matter of taste. What it most certainly is, is imbecilic. It's another in a long line of off-the-cuff remarks that Ann makes, seemingly because she finds it hard not to. It's a compulsion to say something—anything—to make sure the focus stays on her.

In any event, Ann's vituperations about the fairer sex go a long way toward proving her point about women in the military. Lamenting the "disproportionate number of women involved" in the pattern of abuse at Abu Ghraib, Ann calls it yet another lesson on why women shouldn't be soldiers. "In addition to not being able to carry even a medium-sized backpack," she says, "women are too vicious."[10]

Well, *some* women apparently are.

At the risk of slipping into psychobabble, it should be noted that the youngest in a group of siblings, as well as sisters in families that otherwise contain only male children, have a tendency to take on certain characteristics. As psychologist and birth-order expert Kevin Leman explains, last-born children often love the limelight and may be the family clown. But underpinning all the attention seeking is the tendency to be "temperamental, manipulative, spoiled, impatient, and impetuous."[11] In addition to being "suckers for praise and encouragement," last-born children are often natural used-car salesmen—although they do tend to have more success moving lemons off the lot than filling out the necessary paperwork[12] (or, it seems, making clear and accurate attributions when writing). Last-borns are often entertaining and funny, but their weaknesses include being "manipulative, even a little flaky" and "seeming to be too slick," Leman says. They are "prone to talk too much and too long," "push too hard because they see things only their way," can be "a little out of focus—like an airhead," and "may appear self-centered, unwilling to give others credit."[13]

Not that Ann is at all like that. I'm just saying . . .

———

Meanwhile, according to Adlerian psychology, as the youngest in a group of siblings, Ann may want so badly to make it bigger than the others that she develops huge plans that don't come to fruition, all the while remaining the baby of the family. As the only girl, she would likely drift to the extremes of either being hyperfeminine (perhaps with a proclivity to wear cocktail dresses and bleach her long hair) or become a tomboy in an effort to outdo her brothers (maybe—after her sporty high-school years—by following in Father's footsteps and becoming a lawyer). The truth, as they say, is probably somewhere in the middle.

Whatever combination of conditions Ann has struck, she is, to put it mildly, prone to engaging in a sort of mock misogyny that she occasionally takes too far. Either that, or she truly harbors a seething hatred for her own gender. Believers of the latter would likely point to her apotheosizing of Phyllis Schlafly, the grande dame of gender discrimination, whom Ann calls "one of the most accomplished and influential people in America."[14] Given the space afforded to Schlafly in *Slander*, it's no stretch to call Ann a devotee. So one can forgive the overstatement that Schlafly executed a "single-handed defeat of the Equal Rights Amendment."[15] Clearly, Schlafly was a huge driving force in denying women equal rights, but there are very few instances in this country's history of *anyone* single-handedly doing *anything* of that magnitude. Even Jefferson had some help with the Declaration of Independence. Crediting Schlafly to that degree is about on par with believing Al Gore created the Internet.

At the same time, it seems a little disingenuous to say that there is "no important political debate for nearly half a century in which Schlafly's influence has not been felt"[16] and at the same time bewail that the media pays no attention to her. The fact that Schlafly, running as a Republican for an Illinois House seat in 1970, lost to the Democratic incumbent tends to cast just a bit of doubt on her being "one of the most accomplished and influential people in America." (And that was *after* she had written *A Choice, Not an Echo*. She first ran unsuccessfully in 1952.) If losing an election confers such status on a person, then we all should have paid more attention to the sagacious and charming Lyndon LaRouche. Or maybe Barry Goldwater, whom Schlafly helped to garner the 1964 Republican presidential nomination. Maybe, though, the Schlaffster just gets a bad rap from the media because she is so incredibly homophobic despite having a gay son. (It should be noted that Mommy Dearest still lets him work for her.)

Ann also complains that the *New York Times* has never reviewed one of Schlafly's books. Which may be true, but it *has* published a review of a biography about everyone's favorite female woman hater.

In a look at *Phyllis Schlafly and Grassroots Conservatism: A Woman's Crusade* (boy, do conservatives love that word) by Donald T. Critchlow, reviewer Judith Warner points out that Schlafly helped to play up the Equal Rights Amendment as the first step toward the military drafting of girls, unisex bathrooms, and—gasp!—homosexual rights.[17] You know, for people like Schlafly's son.

Warner says this "public relations coup" was the *meisterwerk* of the "clever, charming, ambitious, energetic and forever ladylike woman." While bashing arms limitation, friendly relations with China, and abortion rights (among other seemingly desirable things), Schlafly has "saved special venom for the 'anti-family, anti-children, and pro-abortion' feminist movement," Warner writes. "She opposed the E.R.A. on the grounds that it would take away the 'special protection' the 'Christian tradition of chivalry' offered women—in other words, the 'right' to be 'supported and protected' by men."[18]

Oh, yes—and to make sure we retain gender-segregated rooms in which to answer nature's call.

"Phyllis Schlafly's point that no one wants to end the tradition of separate bathrooms for men and women is so fundamentally true that there is nothing else to be said,"[19] Ann wrote in a column in December 2002. Actually, there's a *lot* left to be said. For one, it's patently *untrue* (does your home have discrete men's and women's rooms?). It also confirms that Ann has been away from New York for too long. Like it or not, it's no surprise to find that your typical small Manhattan bistro these days features unisex toilettes. You know, like in France, "where the practice," lamentably for Ann, "is common."[20]

While calling Schlafly a "remarkable woman," bestselling author and former White House legal counsel to President Nixon John Dean writes that Schlafly's work against the E.R.A. is a "standard authoritarian ploy" (which, by extension, one can assume of Ann's punditry). In his book *Conservatives Without Conscience*, Dean says that Schlafly "relied on fear" and that while "none of [it] was true, her powerful propaganda got the attention of a lot of women who had never been particularly interested in politics."[21] Much the same can be said for Ann. After all, as the teacher, goes the student.

Toward this end, *The New Yorker*'s review of *Phyllis Schlafly and Grassroots Conservatism* (mentioned by Dean) touts the lady's trailblazing tyranny and recognizes the effects on women such as Ann and conservative cohort Laura Ingraham who have taken up the mantle of malice.

"While Ann Coulter and Laura Ingraham were still playing tea party," Elizabeth Kolbert writes, Schlafly "recognized that deliberation was no match for diatribe, and logic no equal to contempt."[22]

———

Schlafly's ardent conservatism clearly informs much of Ann Coulter's worldview, though Ann has raised the hysteria by a few notches. The bottom line is that Ann's idolizing of a woman who thinks that men and women shouldn't have equal rights sort of adds to the idea that Ann is a self-reflexive misogynist. Of course, the signs pointing to that are already pretty overwhelming.

In Ann's world, the dangers in equal rights for both genders lurk not in having to share a lavatory or in military conscription for women. Rather, as is often the case with Ann, the issue is sexual.

"Exhibitionism, promiscuity, sex toys, and adultery. This is women's liberation,"[23] she argues. Jeez. Who knew? That must've been

laid out in a little-known clause tacked on to the end of the amendment. And, as always, it's all liberals' fault.

Liberals "believe in the coarse physical appropriation of women
by men—hookups, trophy wives, strip clubs."[24] Even if that were
true, Ann seems to relish the prospect of being treated like a sex
object. She joked flirtatiously with Leno that if she wanted to
attract people, she would "wear sexy dresses," and "grow [her] hair
long."[25] (Ann, you clever coquette, you.) At the same time, in an
April 1999 whine about how wishy-washy Washington men are
when it comes to wooing women, Ann says she would "take 69
cents on the dollar (or whatever the current feminist myth is) never
to have to ask for a date."[26]

C'mon, now, Ann—it's not as if you're Sadie Hawkins. And even
if you were, it's been almost seventy years since Al Capp made it
okay for her (and all women) to ask guys out. A woman's taking the
romantic initiative isn't a sign of the apocalypse; it's a sign of a free
society. It doesn't denigrate you; it empowers you. Still, maybe it
would help if you put your money where your mouth is and acted
on the "69 cents on the dollar" pledge. Just donate 31 percent of the
$4.9 million you've made on your books—or about a million and a
half—to, say, Habitat for Humanity. It's a near guarantee you'll
wind up with a couple of invitations to dinner and drinks. And
probably from guys who are good with their hands. Manly men—
just your type.

Whether in jest or not, Ann's espousal, so to speak, of the era
before feminism is sexist at best and full of hatred at worst. But it's
her delight in being compared to a man—or to be considered masculine—that really puts the cherry in her old-fashioned.

Ann "cites with great pride a compliment paid by a friend: He told her she wrote like a man," the *Guardian* reported. "He said, 'All of the columnists in the Op-Ed page of the *New York Times* write like women. It's always, 'I was doing such and such today.' And it's all 'feelings' and 'Why do they hate us?' And it takes them, like, four paragraphs to get to the point.' And he said to me, 'You write like a man, just straight in. Point, point, point, point.'"[27]

Pardon my ignorance (and for again slipping into the first person), but I had always figured that telling a woman she's "like a man" is one of the three things you say when you want to make her hate you immediately and irredeemably. In no particular order (because it doesn't matter—any one on the list will do), they are as follows:

> You're a bad mother.
> You're a slut.
> You act like a man.

Naturally, Ann can't legitimately be accused of the first because she has no children. She probably *would* be a bad mother, of course. In fact, she'd probably be the absolute worst—absentee, simultaneously neglectful and domineering, and with nothing but white wine in the fridge. The second possibility was summed up rather neatly by comedian Kathy Griffin. Speaking of Ann's appearance on *Today*, Griffin wondered what kind of a person wears a black cocktail dress at 7 A.M.? Presumably one who dropped by the studio on her way *home*. The old "walk of shame," as they say.

As for her acting like a man, well … that's not really the point, now is it? Glass ceilings remain in this—and just about every other—country. And the irony that they still exist because of people like Ann should not be lost on you. We simply can't have it both ways. We can't expect women to flourish career-wise and then fault them for being ambitious and aggressive. But there's a difference between asserting oneself and reveling in supposed masculinity. And Ann talks a lot about things like "manly honor," especially in contrast to "sobbing hysterical women," the latter of which she refers to as liberals' "doctrine of infallibility."[28] It's as if to show any emotion—or, more accurately, any hint of vulnerability—is unacceptable. No one knows for sure, of course, whether this is a result of Ann's having to fight two older brothers for the last pork chop at the Coulter family table or her emulation of a tough "union-busting" patriarch. And there's certainly nothing wrong with standing up for what you believe and aggressively pursuing what you want. Especially in a country where women still really do make just a fraction of what men do for the same jobs. (It's actually about 75 cents on the dollar, according to a Census Bureau report showing that the disparity widened in 2003.[29]) Especially in a country where, despite some progress, sexual intimidation is a fact of boardroom life and where Geena Davis can't even keep her job as a *fictional* U.S. president.

Despite her penchant for skimpy dresses and lengthy tresses, Ann clearly frowns on femaleness. As she suggested to Sean Hannity, liberals have "managed to eliminate the idea of manly honor. Instead all they have is womanly indignation."[30] In her world, we all just have to suck it up and take the pain. Stoicism is the preferred state. Bite the proverbial bullet. Which goes a long way toward explaining why she thinks it's okay to deliver her message through nasty personal attacks—and why she takes such umbrage at the purported shield around the 9/11 widows. As she says, the truth "cannot be delivered with Novacaine."[31]

Unfailingly, Ann deflects any suggestion that she herself might deal with ad hominem attacks with anything less than her usual aplomb. Her defense typically takes the form of some sort of joke, as it did with Leno:

> **LENO:** Have you ever been hurt by something someone said?
>
> **ANN:** I was wounded when I wrote my "Attack France" column and even liberals didn't mind that one.

How clever.

In fairness, though, when Leno presses Ann on the point, she dispenses with the bons mots. In what seems to be sincerity, she tells Jay of the pride she has in being attacked by her detractors.

> **LENO:** See, you put up a good front. But you know what I'm saying.
>
> **ANN:** Um, no.
>
> **LENO:** You know what I'm saying, seriously. I mean, have you ever went, "Ooh, that person went a little bit too far attacking me," or whatever?
>
> **ANN:** No. I'm—to quote Dan Quayle, one of your other targets—I wear their contempt as a badge of honor.

Setting aside the truly disturbing realization that Jay Leno is a bigger bulldog in his interview with Ann than most journalists have been, it's clear that Ann revels in her own perceived martyrdom. For those of you who remember the SATs, Ann is to the "mainstream media" what Ronald Reagan was (or so she reminds us again and again) to the Soviet Union. She will vanquish the liberal foe while remaining steadfast and imperturbable. Meanwhile, it's the role of liberal women to exert their will through tears and sentiment.

"[N]o woman worth her salt ever loses an argument," Ann asserts. "She starts crying, making it unmanly to pursue your victory."[32] You simply "can't respond to them because that would be questioning the authenticity of their suffering. . . . Victory goes to the most hysterical."[33] Besides, they're so sneaky, these "broads." They'll stop at nothing, which is why it's "not an accident that the relentless attacks on morality spring from America's women."[34] Imagine—going to such lengths as to have your husbands killed in a terrorist attack just so you can come out in support of John Kerry in the 2004 presidential election. It's just absolutely shameless. The next thing you know, they'll be writing letters to the editor of the *Washington Post* saying they were going to break up with their husbands anyway[35]—so there.

In any case, while liberals are prone to "womanly crying" about such things as guns,[36] there are those who say Ann is more than willing to shed a tear, crocodilian or otherwise, in the face of attack. In *Conservatives Without Conscience*, John Dean writes that the steely storm trooper goes a little molten when things get too hot. Dean says Ann is among the conservatives who "love to hurl invective" but "have the thinnest of skins when the same is done to them."[37]

Ann "can trash perceived liberals on national television but has been known to walk offstage when booed, or to start crying when she thinks she is being treated unfairly," Dean writes.[38]

————

Hypocritical or not, it's not just on a personal level that Ann demands we shut up and act like men. As when Ronald Reagan single-handedly dismantled all of the warheads in the Soviet nuclear arsenal with just a ratchet set and a couple of spare hours, we as a country must manifest our destiny regardless of the potential harm we might do to our collective self. We must be the world's John Wayne. And we're talking the Duke, here—the bad-ass one from *True Grit*. After all, we "don't choose the circumstances in which we must exhibit our will as a nation. This is the price of manhood— acting when you must and not complaining that someone might get hurt."[39] It seems that hard-hearted insensitivity to the thousands of twenty-year-olds in the line of fire in Iraq is what is meant by all those "Support the Troops" bumper stickers.

————

This desire not just for patriarchy but outright male-dominated society may help to explain Ann's fondness for men in drag, including what appears to be a sort of obsession with Kabuki theater— you know, the Japanese thing with the real stylized makeup and dancing, where men play all the roles, male and female.[40] It's a reference Ann has made repeatedly, from her infamous September 12,

2001, "kill their leaders" column to her recent appearance on the *Tonight* show.

In any case, Ann's affection for men in hosiery may also give us some insight into why she so hates actresses—Gwyneth Paltrow, in particular. Besides being younger and prettier than Ann, Gwynnie (who, it should be noted, left the University of California at Santa Barbara to pursue her acting career[41])won an Academy Award for her role in *Shakespeare in Love*—in which she played an actress who fought the Elizabethan tradition of having men play all roles onstage. Basically, her character was showbiz's first feminist. And, in the end, she got the guy! What's not to hate?

Still, it's hard to say whether Gwynnie would be one of those women Ann calls "broads"—another term of belittlement that Ann uses a little too often for it to just be a joke or, as she suggests, without connotation. In the face of questioning by master interrogator Jay Leno, who asked her about her use of the word in *Godless*, Ann responded by saying that men "use the word 'broads' all the time to talk about women."[42] Not only is that a cop-out, it's an exaggeration. Maybe in conservative circles "broads" is okay, but it is generally not accepted language in most social and business situations.

Judging by Ann's reasoning, it's fine to pay women less money for the same job because it happens "all the time." Or for construction workers to wolf-whistle at women because it "happens all the time." Or, well, you get the idea.

Ann further dismisses the suggestion that her use of the term is not only offensive but may undermine her ability to make a point, telling Leno that if we get to "that level of parsing my language, there will be no end to this."[43] But it's pretty clear that the objection to the use of the term "broads" is hardly an example of Wittgensteinian linguistic analysis. Simply put, words carry connotations—good and bad. And Ann called a group of women "broads" in an effort to stigmatize them and provoke a reaction. If it's okay, why stop there? Why not call them "bitches"? What about the C-word?

Ann's tearing down of women no doubt betrays her self-loathing. Her body-image issues (explored more fully in "Ann on Sex") suggest that she is simultaneously ashamed of her femininity and yet willing to use it to her advantage. Clearly, Ann Coulter will stop at nothing to play up to the conservative base. She will criticize women for using their attributes, stereotypical or not, to their advantage, and then she will turn around and do the same. Ann Coulter will call women the ugliest names that will get past a newspaper editor just to show how tough she is. But in the end, there are parameters of discourse that, when breached, call into question the underlying point. In Ann's own words, "arguments by demonization . . . can be presumed to be fraudulent."[44]

Chapter 4

Ann on Sex and Abortion

OR

Fetus Don't Fail Me Now

Let's say I go out every night,
I meet a guy and have sex with him.
Good for me. I'm not married.
—ANN speaking on *Rivera Live,* June 7, 2000

Ann Coulter wants nothing more than to see *Roe v. Wade* over-turned, to take away from American women their right to choose. To her, abortion is liberals' holiest sacrament. But it is Ann herself who is completely obsessed with the issue. Huge chunks of *Godless* are little more than the repetition of her stance and demonstrations of how, by contrast, liberals are wrong. And her beliefs go well beyond the standard Christian opposition to abortion. Ann is so militantly antichoice it's a wonder she hasn't yet advocated the bombing of Planned Parenthood clinics.

Meanwhile, Ann's feelings about *Roe v. Wade* to some degree also inform her views on sex. Given her self-righteous and profoundly hypocritical statements about the act, it should come as no surprise that among the men she has been romantically linked to are Bill Maher and Bob Guccione Jr. If the names sound familiar, they should. Maher is a well-known libertarian (some would say liberal) talk-show host and author, and Guccione is the creator and former publisher of *Spin* magazine. Both odd pairings, at first blush. Even odder under closer inspection.

While Maher is despised by much of America's religious right for his criticism of President Bush, his stance against the Iraq war, and his all-around mental acuity, he is often mislabeled as a liberal. In fact, Maher describes himself as a libertarian. He favors partial privatization of Social Security—not to mention the legalization of all drugs (he is a member of the advisory board of NORML—the National Organization for the Reform of Marijuana Laws), prostitution, and pornography. He has also been openly critical of John Kerry and other leading lefties. But beyond some overlap in their views about Democratic ineptitude, Maher and Ann Coulter share the indignity of being fired from jobs for comments made in the wake of the September 11, 2001, terrorist attacks. ABC declined to renew Maher's contract for *Politically Incorrect* in 2002 after he, along with guest conservative political commentator Dinesh D'Souza (another of Ann's reported paramours), objected to the characterization of the men who flew the planes into the World Trade Center's Twin Towers and the Pentagon as cowardly. For that, ABC pulled the plug, though Maher made a comeback and now hosts his own show on HBO.

Ann, meanwhile, got canned from the ultraconservative *National Review,* which dropped her column after she responded to the terrorist attacks by saying that America should "invade their countries, kill their leaders and convert them to Christianity." As the *Guardian* put it, in typically understated British fashion, "getting sacked from [the *National Review*] for being too rightwing takes some doing." Ann reportedly "laughed off" the sacking, calling it "lot of great publicity."[1]

USA Today also removed Coulter as a columnist covering the 2004 Democratic National Convention after she referred to it as the "Spawn of Satan convention."[2] And that's not to mention being fired from her position as a legal correspondent and pundit for MSNBC after she insulted the Vietnam veteran. More recently, at least three newspapers have dropped Ann's syndicated column from their opinion pages in the wake of her comments about the 9/11 widows and charges of plagiarism.

But while common adversity may bring an otherwise unlikely couple together, any chance a Coulter-Maher headline would ever have appeared in the Wedding & Celebrations pages of the *New York Times*'s Sunday style section was probably a long shot: after all, Maher is a self-described environmentalist and thinks religion is a neurological disorder that spreads guilt and hatred. But, hey, not every couple agrees on everything. At the same time, insurmountable obstacles do occasionally crop up. Take, for example, Maher's unbridled (that's a pun, you see) attraction to large-breasted porn stars, such as former girlfriend Heather Hunter.

Hunter—aka, Double H—may be the best-known black porn actress in the world. Now a hip-hop artist and painter (thus rendering her out of Ann's frame of reference on three counts), she could once be found on the arm of Monsieur Maher. One can only imagine the contrast between a six-foot blond sourpuss with the shapeliness of a surfboard who believes nonreproductive sex is a crime against God and man, and a buxom black bombshell who believes nonreproductive sex is how you spend a Saturday afternoon.

At the same time, maybe Ann's not as much of a prude as she seems to be. After all, the aforementioned Bob Guccione Jr. has *his* ties to the sex industry, as well: His father—Bob Guccione Sr., naturally—is the founder and publisher of *Penthouse* magazine. Now, although in the pantheon of porn publishing *Penthouse* may pale in comparison to hard-core pornography, it is nonetheless a magazine that makes hay of lesbianism, onanistic dildo play, and intragender oral sex. Given that Ann thinks award-winning TV show *Sex and the City* is the first sign of the apocalypse, a "classic in the slutty-girl genre,"[3] then surely *Penthouse* is the book of Beelzebub.

But, look—one could argue that Bob Jr. has nothing to do with such filth, and that his now-defunct *Gear* magazine features women who are merely scantily clad rather than naked and penetrated. (In fact, a completely unscientific but thorough study shows that many of the women (di)splayed in *Gear* are wearing more than Ann Coulter does during an appearance on, say, the *Today* show.) But let's not forget that Bob Jr. received about half a million dollars in . . . ahem . . . seed money from dear old dad to jump-start his career in magazine publishing. And how does that jibe with Ann's reference to trailblazing "girlie" magazine magnate Hugh Hefner—the mastermind behind *Playboy* magazine, of course—as a "smut peddler"?[4] Well, frankly, it doesn't.

In any event, Ann seems to have tired of the disheveled devil, despite his personally netting $16.5 million from the sale of *Spin*, his first, and arguably most successful, venture. Consider this 1997 letter to the editor that appeared in the *Washington Post*:

> *I must write to correct a few of the many egregious misstatements in your ... Reliable Source column. I am not, and have never been arm candy for Bob Guccione Jr. The Gooch was my arm candy—my boy toy—whom I eventually, and regretfully, had to replace with a much younger man.*
>
> —*Ann Coulter*

Umm ... okay.

———

Anyway, perhaps more relevant to Ann's views on sex than the debate about who was the weak link in that daisy chain is her apparent jealousy. Oh, sure—she may contend that "The Gooch" wasn't young and pretty enough for her, but how can we be sure? After all, Bob Guccione Jr. has also dated columnist and *Sex and the City* creator Candace Bushnell. Now, whether or not you've ever seen the show, the title alone ought to tell you what you need to know about it. We're talking about the woman whose erotic exploits have informed the sex lives of millions of American women for much of the past decade. Let's face it, it's tough to follow Bushnell in the romance department. Those are some big Jimmy Choos to fill.

But, hey—maybe Ann's hatred of 1) women, 2) Manhattanite women, and 3) Manhattanite women with fulfilling and enriching sex lives isn't sour grapes at all. Maybe she deserves the benefit of the doubt when she refers to the "grim, quivering, angry women on the Upper West Side"[5] who write letters to the editor of the *New York Times.* As opposed to those who write letters to the *Washington Post* on life-and-death matters such as who broke up with whom.

Either way, it must really burn Ann's breeches when a British newspaper—in an article proudly displayed on Ann's Web site, anncoulter.org, incidentally—calls her "a Manhattan blonde with dating worries and enough acid one-liners to blow the Manolo Blahniks off the *Sex and the City* gang." And to drive the point further home, to say that, "like Carrie, *Sex and the City*'s fictional columnist, Coulter says she likes to write at home, dressed in her underwear." [6]

Of course, maybe the *Guardian* was going hard on Ann in response to such blatantly Anglophobic—not to mention misogynistic—comments as this, made on MSNBC shortly after the death of Princess Diana, in September 1997: "Her children knew she's sleeping with all these men. That just seems to me, it's the definition of 'not a good mother.' ... Is everyone just saying here that it's OK to ostentatiously have premarital sex in front of your children? ... [Diana is] ordinary and pathetic and confessional—I've never had bulimia! I've never had an affair! I've never had a divorce! So I don't think she's better than I am."

It's true that Ann has never been married. If serial betrothal and breakup is any indication, she lacks the commitment. While Ann casts aspersions on those who have suffered a divorce, she has been engaged at least three times—or "something like that," she told *Time* magazine. In addition to having been to "dozens" of Dead shows back in the day, the so-called spindle-shanked blonde also typically attends the Halloween parade of drag queens in Greenwich Village.[7]

Regardless, Ann seems to have had at least a passing obsession with eating disorders. The "bulimia" denial came shortly after she said—on ex-boyfriend Bill Maher's *Politically Incorrect,* perhaps in an effort to persuade him of her own mental health—that girls who suffer from anorexia "never have boyfriends. . . . That's one way to know you don't have anorexia: if you have a boyfriend."[8] Meanwhile, countless Web sites speculate that Ann, herself, suffers from some form of eating disorder. It should be noted that there is no evidence of this aside from the fact that at a towering six feet tall, she weighs south of a hundred pounds. No surprise, given that she has admitted to spending much of her twenties taking nourishment from little other than Chardonnay and cigarettes.[9] On top of that, actress Calista Flockhart, no stranger to allegations of suffering from anorexia, is set to play a conservative newspaper columnist based loosely on Ann this fall. At the same time, the show's producer, Ken Olin, told *Editor & Publisher* that Flockhart's character is "not Ann Coulter. She's not insane."[10]

At any rate, Ann's infatuation with eating disorders seems to have given way to her newest bugaboo: the sexual act known as "fisting," which warrants no fewer than three mentions in *Godless*—but, curiously, does not appear in the index.

Perhaps the most egregious of the references comes early in the book when, in a rant she will take up in full in the later chapter about education, she asserts that "[l]iberals used to tell us they were teaching fisting to fourth-graders because 'kids are going to have sex anyway!'"[11] Thankfully, Ann's lack of attribution for that statement (in a book that has more than three hundred endnotes) is all the proof the reader needs that it is absurd to its core. The only possible way for anyone to believe a statement so ridiculous and inflammatory is to find a liberal—or even a convicted serial killer, for that matter—who advocates fourth graders' engaging in fisting. And even if such a thing does get mentioned in sex-ed classes, surely someone of Ann's astounding acumen knows there's a huge difference between explaining to someone what something is and promoting it as a desirable course of action. Or should the New Testament be considered a how-to guide for killing supposed messiahs?

Arguing against this purported Caligulan curriculum, Ann offers up the admittedly abominable tale of Chelmsford (Massachusetts) High School's hiring of a woman by the name of Suzi Landolphi to deliver an AIDS-awareness speech. Ann describes Landolphi's ninety-minute presentation as including lewd language, a comment to a student that would be considered sexual harassment in most places of business, and the request that students "show their 'orgasm faces' in front of a camera."[12] But Ann takes most umbrage, ultimately, with Landolphi's looks.

"Like most people who enjoy talking to strangers about sex," Ann says, "Landolphi, to put it as charitably as possible, is physically repulsive in appearance."[13] Beyond the redundancy of Ann's assertion that this woman is physically repulsive "in appearance" (how else can you be "physically repulsive" but "in appearance"?), what are we to make of the fact that Ann, herself, spends a good chunk of her professional life "talking to strangers about sex"? Unless, of course, she considers her readers to be friends and acquaintances.

And what bearing are we to assume attractiveness—or, at least, Ann's determination of it—has on anyone's ability to speak authoritatively about sex? Does hotness validate one's scholarship on the subject?

Either way, if she has followed her own rules about the evils of nonreproductive carnal relations, then an unmarried, childless paragon of purity such as Saint Ann has never *had* sex. Ever. (And that would include, naturally, the mortal sin of masturbation.) And if by some miracle that's true, why would *any* thinking human being take advice about sex from someone who has never had it? That would be like asking Father Quinlan for tips on finding your girlfriend's G-spot.

More realistically, it seems fairly obvious that Ann Coulter *has* had sex—and doesn't lack for suitors. Even so, we've seen that her choices of partners can run counter to her stated preference for "fearsome" conservative men. Questioned by Jay Leno during her June 14, 2006, appearance on *The Tonight Show,* Ann (in an obvious joke) claimed never to have slept with a liberal. Leno suggested that she should try it to see what it's like. Ann replied that she had "read about it in *Esquire,* and it does not sound good."

Which is a pretty funny line, but offers very little insight at all. And so we're left focusing on the men she has been linked to in various media reports. Counterbalancing conservatives like D'Souza are men such as Christopher Putala.

Putala was mentioned in a January 31, 2004, article in the *Washington Post* that examined John Kerry's fund-raising during his presidential campaign. The *Post* reported that Putala, a lobbyist for the Cellular Telecommunications and Internet Association, was "among Kerry's biggest presidential fundraisers."[14] Whether or not he's a bona fide liberal is open to speculation, of course, given what he does for a living. Nonetheless, his helping to finance Ann's sworn enemy mustn't be overlooked. It's one thing to have voted for Kerry, quite another to have handed him tens of thousands of dollars in campaign money.

But love is proverbially blind. Besides, politics be damned, the guy is really good-looking. In a photo essay about Ann on the *Time* magazine Web site, Putala is shown besuited and glancing smolderingly over his shoulder, cigar in hand, while Ann looks smilingly on. In the caption for the undated photo, which was given to *Time* by Ann and taken in Washington, Putala is described as "an ex" and— yes, it's true—a Democrat.[15]

Somewhat disturbingly, Putala also bears a striking resemblance to a young Alec Baldwin. Seriously, he does. Slicked-back hair, chiseled jawline, strong nose. It's uncanny. And weird, given that Baldwin is one of Ann's staunchest Hollywood nemeses. So at odds are Ann and Alec that the two recently engaged in a bit of a media feud.

For an article in *Elle* magazine, Baldwin was asked, apropos of younger brother Stephen's converting to conservatism, whether he (Alec) would rather sleep with Dianne Feinstein or Ann. He replied that he'd have to go with the sixty-three-year-old Democratic senator from California because with Ann, "we'd have sex and I'd have to jump out the window."[16]

Responding in Lloyd Grove's "Lowdown" column in the New York *Daily News,* Ann got the upper hand in the media feud, saying that the actor's ensuing suicide would be "the only reason I can think of for wanting to have sex with Alec Baldwin."[17]

Sure, it was no Britney-Justin spat, but it'll do. Let's just be thankful there were no kids involved. Of course, if Ann Coulter and Alec Baldwin ever *did* act on whatever sexual tension they may share, Ann's anti-abortion stance would add to the odds for offspring.

Not coincidentally, much of Ann's obsession with sex involves the potential for abortion and, typically, Democrats' defense of a woman's right to it. The legion of pro-choice Republicans generally escape Ann's wrath, of course. Though, in true schoolgirl-crush fashion, she has said that former New York mayor and ardent abortion-rights proponent Rudy Giuliani is the only "prominent pro-choice Republican who has ever demonstrated that he does have the guts and IQ to stand up to media attacks."[18]

To Ann, "[t]he Democrats' only hope is to lie and pretend they stand for something other than the right of women to have unprotected sex with men they don't like"[19]—a ridiculous statement she soon echoes by alleging that Democrats want merely to "preserve the right of women to have sex with men whose babies they don't want to carry."[20] Presumably, she means men like Bill Maher and "The Gooch."

Meanwhile, Ann may have some splainin' to do in her next book regarding the conservative squeeze being put on some so-called pregnancy resource centers. It seems that pressure to get federal funding may be pushing the centers to offer misleading information about the health risks associated with abortion. According to an Associated Press report on July 17, 2006, congressional aides posing as teenagers called twenty-five pregnancy centers that had received government funding in the past five years and were told of "the increased risk for cancer, infertility and stress disorders."[21]

The report, prepared for Congressman Henry Waxman, a Democrat from California, showed that despite inconclusive evidence that abortion raises a woman's risk of cancer, at least one center told the aide who called that the risk could be as much as 80 percent higher, while the Web site of another center claims that it could increase by half. Only a "small fraction of the more than 4,000 pregnancy clinics nationwide get any federal funding," the AP report said. Most of them "for promoting sexual abstinence."[22]

It seems that saying Democrats' "only hope is to lie" might more appropriately be said of those on the other side of the abortion divide.

Whether Ann, in her anti-abortion vehemence, favors such misinformation and scare tactics is a matter for speculation. But let's not forget that we're talking about a lawyer who helped Paula Jones with her case against President Clinton and whose first book was called *High Crimes and Misdemeanors—The Case Against Bill Clinton*. No surprise, then, that much of her rage/sexual frustration is directed at our forty-second president, who, as of July 2001, had been mentioned in seventeen of her twenty-eight columns.[23]

Ann has never lacked for something bad to say about Clinton. Among her tasteless televised comments include the notion that Clinton was fond of masturbating in the White House sinks[24] and is "in love with the erect penis."[25]

Everyone is entitled to an opinion (though, the first of those two statements seems more or less meant to be taken as a fact). But when those opinions are then twisted and misrepresented, it qualifies as bad journalism.

Take the following passage, from page 25 of *Slander*:

In polls—considered determinative on most matters by Democrats—80 percent of respondents who heard [Juanita] Broaddrick's allegations thought they were true (62 percent) or possibly true (18 percent). Only 20 percent of respondents did not believe Broaddrick's assertion that a sitting United States president committed rape.

Her attribution for this statistic? A Fox News poll.

The relevance of this statistic breaks down on two fronts. The first can be found in the misleading statement that only a fifth of respondents "did not believe" Broaddrick's allegations—the implication being that a full four-fifths *did* believe her. A closer look at the wording shows that the 38 percent who merely thought it "possibly true" shouldn't be lumped in with those who were certain. After all, opinions aside, it's "possibly true" that Dick Cheney died of a massive coronary in 2002 and is merely being carted around—à la *Weekend at Bernie's*—by Karl Rove and his staff. It's "possibly true" that *High Crimes and Misdemeanors* was written by one of an infinite number of monkeys sitting at an infinite number of typewriters. Well, okay—probably not. But it's "possibly true" that George W. Bush was negligent in his duties as a member of the Alabama National Guard. Just because something is "possibly true" doesn't make it true.

Secondly, the results are from respondents to Fox News poll! And while Ann may believe that Fox "isn't even particularly conservative,"[26] the rest of us should nonetheless be shocked that only about three out of five of respondents to a poll conducted by a "news" agency that puts Sean Hannity on the air believed Broaddrick. That's pretty low, considering a bigger majority of those very same people probably still believe that Iraq was behind the attacks of 9/11.

———

Meanwhile, Ann's belief that being pro-choice and being pro-abortion are the same thing is about on par with saying that you either support the right of bars to exist and are therefore an alcoholic, or you think drinking establishments should be outlawed, which makes you a teetotaler. While in many cases either of those may be true, the conditions arbitrarily assume a binary state. That is to say, it doesn't leave room for the possibility that somewhere, in the tens of thousands of pubs, taverns, inns, and watering holes that litter this great country, there is someone soberly sipping a soda. But Ann's misrepresentations don't stop with liberals (by which, she of course means Democrats). After a classic misdirection in which she says the Republican Party "was founded expressly as the antislavery party, which to a great extent remains their position today"[27]—a statement that is irrelevant and not quite true—she contrasts Republicans and Democrats by saying Republicans are the "Blacks-Aren't-Property/Don't-Kill-Babies party. They're the Hookup party."[28]

Funny, then, how she goes on to rail against two Senate votes on a bankruptcy bill featuring an amendment that would have excluded protesters at abortion clinics from bankruptcy protection. "The amazing thing," she writes "is that the abortion amendment to the bankruptcy bill actually was approved by the Senate in 2003 and was only narrowly defeated in the Senate in 2005, by a 53–46 vote."[29] Given the Republican majority that has been in place in the Senate since 2003, it seems pretty apparent that at least some Republicans may not be voting the way Ann would like them to. So much for the "Don't-Kill-Babies party" slogan.

———

Ann tries to assign blame for the continued legality of abortion and Senate votes that don't go her way on the disparity between campaign contributions made by pro-choice and anti-choice groups, saying that the fund-raising group Emily's List raised $34 million for pro-choice candidates in 2004, while the National Right to Life Committee raised only about $1.7 million.[30] Chalking up the difference to pro-choice "zealots [who] demand that the Democrats swear absolute fealty to their craziest positions," Ann doesn't stop to consider that maybe pro-choice groups have an easier time raising money because *most Americans are pro-choice.* In fact, Ann herself provides the statistic for you, on page 91, when she quotes Senator Dianne Feinstein, fresh from her success in the Alec Baldwin Sweepstakes, as saying that "[t]he American people are—according to the latest ABC poll—60 percent supportive of *Roe.*"[31] Admittedly, in these days of Katherine Harris, hanging chads, and the suppression of the black vote, the majority doesn't always win the day. Especially in Ann's home state of Florida. But in most places, 60 percent is still a majority (another concept Ann has a little trouble grasping. See her comments about voting majorities in the chapter "Ann Speaks"). Highlighting the fact that most Americans want abortion to remain legal doesn't do much in the way of supporting your idea that it shouldn't.

Then again, maybe it's only a matter of time until people start seeing things Ann's way. After all, to Ann, it's "easy to imagine" a person's conversion from pro-choice to anti-abortion "based on new information—ultrasounds, medical advances, pictures of babies smiling in the womb."[32]

British broadcaster and publisher Sky News reported in September of 2003 that "astonishing images" produced by a new scanning technique showed fetuses "apparently smiling and crying."[33] The "discovery" was made by a doctor at the Create Health Centre for Reproduction and Advanced Technology, whose Web site features testimonials about the new technique and a list of fees for prospective customers who want to see their children "smiling" in utero. As Ellie Lee pointed out in her "Ethical Issues" column on the U.K.'s Pro-Choice Forum the day after reports of the "remarkable" discovery, "[a]s most people understand, the expression of emotions and feelings (a crucial aspect of what it means to be a person) requires some development of the self. Just because a fetus moves its facial muscles and curves its lips does not mean it is 'smiling' in any real sense of the word."[34]

Lee chalks up anti-abortion crusaders' jumping on this piece of "evidence" to "just how out of touch with women's experience of pregnancy they are." She says it is "wishful thinking on the part of those opposed to abortion to imagine that pictures of fetuses, however much they 'smile,' [or] 'wave' . . . will lead to abortion being restricted by law or rejected by women."

It's probably no stretch to agree with Lee that promoting the idea of smiling babies indicates a bit of a tenuous grasp on reality. Meanwhile, Ann attacks Democrats for pointing out that the word "abortion" doesn't appear in the Bible—which, she admits, it doesn't. Her counterargument? "It doesn't have words like *child rape,* either, but that doesn't mean Christianity is ambiguous on the subject." (Well, no, it's not. Just ask any Catholic altar boy.) Again, this is a typical Coulterian argument—point out a perceived flaw in the other side's reasoning in an effort to lend your argument credibility. Ann should worry a little less about abortion and a little more about carrying her arguments to full term.

————

Related to Ann's antichoice stance is her opposition to embryonic-stem-cell research. "Liberals lie about the science on stem-cell research," Ann writes, "because they warm to the idea of destroying human embryos."[35] Let's be honest here: Ann Coulter can't possibly believe that liberals get their jollies from destroying human embryos. It's simply not a possibility. Which, unfortunately for her, makes it all the easier to dismiss her stance as political opportunism. Rightfully or not, Republicans—from George W. Bush to the greenest congressman—have turned embryonic stem cells into a political pigskin (if you'll pardon the gruesome imagery).

Bush, of course, used his first veto to shoot down a bill that would have provided more federal money for embryonic-stem-cell research. In a letter to the House of Representatives, he wrote that if the bill were to become law, "American taxpayers for the first time in our history would be compelled to fund the deliberate destruction of human embryos."[36]

In all likelihood, Ann was ecstatic about the president's bold stand. In her world, "the idea that embryonic stem cells are on the verge of curing anything is absurd."[37] But even Ann's beloved Fox News reluctantly admits that "[m]any scientists say the embryonic stem cells hold more hope than their adult-derived counterparts because they are the cells that multiply into the types of cells that build the human body. Adult stem cells do not act the same way."[38]

Of course, Ann also contends that research on both embryonic and adult stem cells has been going on "since the fifties," while saying that embryonic-stem-cell researchers "have not even begun one human clinical trial."[39] Whether or not that's true (and how can anyone be sure, given the conspicuous lack of attribution?), the implication that scientists need to kill babies to study and test embryonic stem cells is simply false.

In Ann's view, "[s]tem-cell research is an even worse excuse for the slaughter of life than abortion."[40] But in fact, proponents of embryonic-stem-cell research—including such disparate enthusiasts as Republican first lady for the ages Nancy Reagan and bestselling writer/philosopher Sam Harris—know that "the embryos in question will have been cultured in vitro (not removed from a woman's body)."[41] But forget Nancy—after all, as Ann points out in *Godless*, while in the White House, Mrs. Reagan used to consult astrologers about her husband's schedule, which made her ripe for ridicule and so maybe she shouldn't be trusted about matters of science.[42] (Incidentally, Ann also recycles a bit of her own material there, talking about how when Mrs. Reagan came out in support of the research, liberals wanted to anoint her "Seer of Technology," a one-liner that first appeared in a column of Ann's from June 16, 2004.) So, fine, we'll stick with Harris, whose *The End of Faith* won the 2005 PEN Award for nonfiction—and who, it should be noted, not only agrees with Ann's view that America is "at war with

Islam,"[43] but also has argued that the torture of prisoners may not only be ethically sound but militaristically pragmatic.[44]

"We know that much can be learned from research on embryonic stem cells," Harris writes. Meanwhile, opponents of embryonic-stem-cell research "believe that even a human zygote [a fertilized egg] should be accorded all the protection of a fully developed human being. But . . . as much can be said of almost every cell in the human body. By the measure of a cell's *potential,* whenever the president scratches his nose he is now engaged in a diabolical culling of souls."[45]

But believing that a cell—or thousands, *millions* of cells—on the tip of the president's Pinocchial proboscis is worth less, cosmically speaking, than a single zygote in the moment after conception is immaterial to the debate. On top of the ability to culture the cells in question in test tubes, preventing their study won't change the fact that abortion in the United States *is still legal*—thus rendering the attack that "liberals just want to kill humans"[46] misguided, if politically expedient.

Or is it?

———

Just after the president's veto of the bill, the *Wall Street Journal* posited that the stem-cell issue could hurt Republicans in the midterm election in November 2006. "While Mr. Bush's position cheers religious and social conservatives in the Republicans' base, nationwide it has alienated many moderates and has some questioning their fealty to a party increasingly defined by its cultural conservatism in emphasizing its opposition to issues such as gay marriage and abortion," the *Journal* said. At the same time, polls show the "president's position is a minority one, even among Republicans." [47]

At any rate, Ann seems happier in shooting down the value of embryonic-stem-cell research than in dealing with abortion. After all, at least she doesn't have to hear the "stories of women carrying the babies of rapists—as if that's happened more than twice in the last half century."[48]

Well, if you're going to deride women who were widowed on 9/11, you might as well throw those who have been sexually assaulted into the mix. Which, again, is a typical Ann Coulter argument. Rather than back up her statements with unassailable, or at least somewhat defensible, supporting evidence, she simply spews sarcasm. With regard to sex, Ann Coulter's hypocrisy is undeniable. Her avoidance of a stance on birth control is conspicuous, to say the least—especially given her dating habits in the context of her claims to Christian conservatism. Abortion and stem-cell research are the current political climate's cash cows of controversy, and so Ann is content to milk them for all they're worth. She is too wrapped up in the *politics* of sex to make clear her own position. In fact, her fierce privacy makes her guilty of the very thing she uses to castigate people like Cindy Sheehan and the 9/11 widows: absolute moral authority. No one, it seems, is allowed to question Ann's duplicity. But "do as I say, not as I do" is a parental truncheon, not a viable political stance. At some point, informed voters need to stand up and point out that the emperor has no clothes. It seems sensible to start with the self-appointed Lady Godiva[49] of conservativism.

Chapter 5

Ann on Religion
OR
There's Only "Right" and Wrong

I'm not God, I don't decide who goes to Hell.
All I can do is live my life according to my understanding
of what God wants of me.
—ANN COULTER **in the** *Guardian*

Much of the recent criticism leveled at those on the religious right takes aim at the hypocrisy of many of its members. The incongruity of promoting Christian compassion while cutting public-assistance budgets. The preaching of virtue and acceptance while engaging in a politicized movement toward intolerance. In short, there are those who have opened themselves up to denunciation because of their simultaneous sanctimony and subjugation of vast segments of society. Claiming to stand for Christian charity while denying basic health care to the working poor is shameful. Worse yet is the pretense of patriotism in the "all men are created equal" mode—that is, unless you're gay or an immigrant. It's the false faith in God and the Founding Fathers that is so troubling. And not just for the pedophilic priest or the thieving theocrat. On a much simpler level, this country is rife with those who do not practice what they preach. Whether Ann is worthy of such dubious distinction seems pretty apparent so far. After all, this is a woman who contends that nonreproductive sex is sinful but thinks it's okay for her to "go out every night . . . meet a guy and have sex with him." This is a woman who claims to be a "very serious" Christian[1] and yet promotes the idea of the death penalty for homosexuals[2] (all the while having friends who are gay). And so it's particularly troubling when she spouts, as an attack on liberals, things like "[i]nstead of transcendent moral values, the Darwinian ethic said all morals are relative."[3]

Perhaps it's impolite to point out the obvious, but *of course* morality is relative—and that has nothing at all to do with Darwin. Humanity's moral values are anything but "transcendent." Our sense of right and wrong is entirely dependent on such things as geography, technology, the age in which we live, how much money we have as a society—all manner of circumstances.

Don't believe it? Just picture a woman guest on Jack Paar's *The Tonight Show* wearing a minidress the likes of which Ann sported for her appearance on *Leno*. It wouldn't happen. Better yet, picture a Muslim woman walking down Main Street in Tehran wearing that dress instead of a burka. Now, you can make the hairsplitting argument that those are *ethical* or *behavioral* issues rather than *moral* ones, but the bottom line is that our sense of right and wrong—and how to act accordingly—is continually evolving. As such, looking for transcendent morality in a two-millennium-old work of fiction is an exercise in futility. As Sam Harris put it in *The End of Faith*, "[i]f there are right and wrong answers to ethical questions, these answers will be best sought in the living present.... The pervasive idea that religion is somehow the *source* of our deepest ethical intuitions is absurd. We no more get our sense that cruelty is wrong from the pages of the Bible than we get our sense that two plus two equals four from the pages of a textbook on mathematics."[4]

When it comes to religion—and especially evolution and the teaching of "intelligent design"—Ann's modus operandi is to charge that liberals can do nothing but make unsupportable assertions and then point to them as the final word. The fact is, no one is guiltier of this than she. With equally bold and ridiculous statements such as "[l]iberal doctrines are less scientifically provable than the story of Noah's ark,"[5] it's difficult to take any related claims seriously.

The assertion that without the belief that we are "moral beings in God's image," we "risk being lured into misguided pursuits, including bestiality, slavery, and PETA membership"[6] may have a nice punch line, but a decent joke doesn't a truth make. If it did, we would have had a Jewish president by now. But leaving aside the levity, Ann's point seems to be that our society's move away from religious doctrine—specifically the Old and New Testaments—as our set of guiding principles is the first step on our collective road trip to perdition. Obviously, this doesn't leave much room for Muslims or—heaven forbid—atheists. Moreover, it doesn't allow for *any* changeability, despite the enjoyment by people like Ann of modern developments such as birth control, Chardonnay, and shifting hemlines. Instead, aptly named blind faith is the path to mythical salvation. Which would be fine, if Ann were a true follower. But her "invade their countries, kill their leaders and convert them to Christianity" idea doesn't quite scream tolerance in any "turn the other cheek" way. Nor does calling Kanye West an animal for speaking his mind. And forget California's (admittedly misguided) "three strikes and you're out." Saint Peter asks that you forgive seventy times seven times.

One of Ann's earliest criticisms in *Treason* is of liberals' "Rousseauian respect for Third World Savages."[7] But simply put, Ann's morality—our morality—is a lot more Rousseauian than Christian, whether or not she wants to admit it. In fact, much of the allegedly small-government conservative movement rather strictly adheres to ideas laid out by the Frenchman (or, as the U.S. Congress will surely soon decree, the "Freedom" man) in the time leading up to the democratic revolutions in France and the then American colonies.

In the introduction to Barnes & Noble's edition of *The Social Contract*, political science scholar Alissa Ardito points out that Rousseau believed that the "common good takes precedence over individual preference,"[8] which could be seen as bolstering Ann's support for racial profiling in airport-security lines. On top of that, the *Contract* promotes the idea that "genuine self-government . . . is possible only in cities or small states,"[9] which hews closely to conservatives' feelings for the United Nations and other global governing bodies. Finally, the belief that "[p]eople can vanquish chaos by working together to preserve their lives, liberty, and property"[10] sounds a lot like the guiding principle of the Conservative Golden Age, the 1950s.

There's no denying, however, that the *Social Contract* is far more convoluted with nuance than that. We simply can't pare it down to the sorts of sound bites that conservatives rely so heavily on ("he's a flip-flopper"; "teach the controversy"). But the point, as Rousseau shows us, is that religion is not a prerequisite for a society to exist as a moral and ethical one.

Again, though, pitting Ann against a 250-year-old work, no matter how seminal, seems somewhat silly. Even with the increased popularity conferred by death (has Ray Charles ever moved more records?), Jean-Jacques probably doesn't sell as many books these days as Ann does. At the risk of confusing sales with influence or importance, and thus discounting the difference between serious philosophy and simpleminded polemics, we should probably keep things a little more contemporary—if only to satisfy Sam Harris's condition that answers to ethical questions are "best sought in the living present."

In *Darwin's Dangerous Idea*, a finalist for the 1995 National Book Award, Daniel C. Dennett examines the difficulty faced by those seeking moral and ethical guidance in the context of evolutionary biology. Acknowledging that Darwin's theory "has been abused and misrepresented by friend and foe alike . . . misappropriated to lend scientific respectability to appalling political and social doctrines,"[11] Dennett steps unflinchingly forward into the fray. While the theory of evolution "cuts much deeper into the fabric of our most fundamental beliefs than many of its sophisticated apologists have yet admitted, even to themselves," we mustn't simply fall back into belief in the divine merely because it's comforting, he says. "The kindly God who lovingly fashioned each and every one of us . . . is, like Santa Claus, a myth of childhood, not anything a sane, undeluded adult could literally believe in. *That* God must either be turned into a symbol for something less concrete or abandoned altogether."[12] In short, there is "no future in a sacred myth."[13]

At the same time, no one is arguing that it's easy to abandon the basis for what has been eons of codified morality while seeking to preserve the morality itself. In fact, the Christian "Golden Rule" of doing unto others as you would have them do unto you is a pretty sound piece of advice—one we might want to hold on to no matter which side of the deistic divide you fall into. Ditto the Ten Commandments. Moreover, it might serve us better if we agreed that such guidelines should be heeded because of their continuing pertinence rather than simply because they've been around a long time. *Stare decisis* aside, precedence doesn't mean much when it comes to morality. Continually re-evaluating the applicability of our behavioral principles seems a much more reasonable way to go. Which lends particular relevance to Ann's desire to subject the justices on the U.S. Supreme Court to a polygraph to determine whether or not they are truly atheists. She dreams of asking each of them if they "believe in a Higher Being? . . . No, seriously."[14] In the end, it shouldn't matter.

Meanwhile, maintaining that a behavioral code should be based on the tenets of Christian mythology while seeking the immunity to stretch the acceptable limits of that behavior is hypocrisy in its purest form. Saving the really significant subliminal-suggestion stuff for later, a quick peek at the cover of *Godless* is fairly telling. In the photo, Ann is wearing a bejeweled cross on a chain around her neck and a dress that would prevent her from entering most churches in Rome by virtue of its showing too much of her shoulders. It's a very wholesome/whore Madonna-esque (the singer) dichotomy, emblematic of Ann's "the rules don't apply to me" stance on most matters.

But how serious a Christian is Ann, really? The *Guardian* asked her that very question in 2003. In typical fashion, Ann answered with a snide remark. "Christianity is even more important to me than homosexuality is to liberals—which apparently comes in a close second to defending Saddam Hussein and preaching anti-Semitism," she said.[15]

At the same time, she claims that the "religious right" is apocryphal—that "the very phrase is a meaningless concept."[16] In short, there ain't no such thing. Which doesn't explain why Ann is so keen to point to the disparity in votes for George Bush between those who regularly attend religious services and those who do not. As she writes in *How to Talk to a Liberal,* the independent Pew Research Center for the People and the Press released a "poll showing that people who regularly attend religious services supported Bush 63 percent to 37 percent, and those who never attend religious services opposed him 62 percent to 38 percent."[17]

To recap: There's no such thing as the religious right—an entity that, by the way, supports President Bush in droves.

———

It's just another example of Ann's tendency to say or write whatever she thinks will provoke outrage. To Ann, the suggestion that there is a religious right just demonstrates how alarmist liberals are.

"[I]t shows the ideological insanity of these people and how they are terrified of anyone who believes in a Being even higher than the

New York Times," she told Pat Robertson on *The 700 Club* in October 2002. "When you try to figure out what the 'religious right' is, essentially my conclusion is that it either comes down to one man, Pat Robertson, or 80 percent of Americans—anyone who believes in God and wants his taxes cut. When you look at Pat Robertson's positions, they are really quite moderate positions, as one would expect from a Yale Law School graduate.

"It really shows how crazy these people are," she continued, not sounding insane herself in any way at all. "They really are terrified of believing Christians."[18]

According to Ann, that terror has culminated in the outlawing of monotheistic belief across America, even as schoolchildren are force-fed the "religion" of liberalism. She contends that a Martian landing in America would conclude that "Christianity and Judaism are prohibited by law. And not just in Cambridge, Massachusetts, where it's actually on the books."[19]

This is a perfect example of Ann's misleading statements, much like the one about how liberals charged "John Ashcroft of essentially belonging to the Klan." (See "Ann Speaks" for the full story on the Ashcroft fabrication.) Given that Ann, in a shock to all involved, doesn't attribute the assertion, it seemed that a conversation with someone at Cambridge City Hall was needed to see if she was right.

After I had left a message with his assistant, Mayor Kenneth Reeves returned my call, and we had a quick chat. I explained to him that Ann Coulter had written in *Godless* that his town was a leading culprit in the persecution of those who practice a religion. When that didn't elicit much of a response, I asked if there was *any* relevant ordinance on the books in Cambridge that prohibited Judaism, Christianity, or any other religion. An apparently matter-of-fact fellow, Reeves said, simply, "Not to my knowledge."

"Any idea what she might be referring to?" I asked.

"No," he said. "I think that's a bold assertion without any basis."

"Do you think maybe it's just her trying to highlight the fact that Cambridge is a hotbed of liberalism?" I asked.

Reeves admitted that Cambridge "probably *is* that." And that's when I thought I had him, the godless heathen. And just as I was about to unleash, he added, "But I don't think it has removed religion in any way."

"Oh—okay," I said. "Well, ummm . . . thanks for calling me back."

But still, there must be something to Ann's assertion. Surely, a look at the Cambridge, Massachusetts, municipal code would show it. The section of the city's Web site listing ordinances[20] is pretty easy to find. There's probably something on there about crèches or menorahs and the public display thereof. Or maybe Christmas caroling. Surely that's at least a misdemeanor.

Here's a partial list of what *is* prohibited (on public property) in Cambridge:

- Cleaning or shaking out of carpets or rugs
- Damaging flower beds
- Shooting a gun (except in the performance of legal duty)
- Littering
- Skateboarding (except in designated areas)

Hmm . . . nothing about Nativity scenes, dreidels, or off-key singing. But maybe it's just an implied prohibition. No need for a law because people know not to practice any religion in Cambridge. Oddly, a Yahoo! search turns up eighty-six churches and two temples/synagogues in the city. Hard to believe that there's only one mosque, though, given that Islam is apparently legal—and besides, we all know that mosques are the best place for liberals to harbor the terrorists they love so much. In all, there are 104 religious organizations in Cambridge. Given all those outlaws, that place must be like the Wild West. Or worse—the Wild Upper West Side of Manhattan.

———

When in Manhattan, Ann insulates herself from the heathens living above West Fifty-ninth Street by attending Redeemer Presbyterian on Broadway in midtown.[21] Or has at least once, anyway. Whether Ann is devout or her visit to Redeemer was merely for show is a matter of some debate. But in any case, she was accompanied there for a service by *Time*'s John Cloud, who reported that the church's senior pastor, the Reverend Tim Keller, spoke of "the importance of allowing one's heart to be 'melted by the sense of God's grace because of what He did on the cross for you.'"

Seems like pretty good advice, whether or not you believe it's divinely inspired. Unfortunately for Ann's acquaintances—especially those who are gay—she seems disinclined to heed it. Asked by *Time*'s Cloud about the possibility that Christian conservatives would regard the sexual orientation of her gay family and friends as an "abomination," Ann answered by saying that it wasn't up to her whether they spent eternity down below—and we're not talking about Australia.

"I'm not God, I don't decide who goes to Hell," she said. "All I can do is live my life according to my understanding of what God wants of me, and—as luck would have it—I'm not a lesbian."[22]

What open arms. What a level of acceptance. That's about as tolerant as you'd expect a Parisian waiter to be with a family of shorts-wearing American rubes who think the French term for "please" is pronounced "silver plate." Meanwhile, as our protagonista herself might phrase it: a Yahoo! search turned up no reports contradicting the belief that Ann disagrees with the tolerance espoused by Redeemer's Reverend Keller.

A call to the church to get a feel for the faith of its perhaps most infamous attendee wasn't as fruitful as first hoped. As this was being written, Keller was on sabbatical, as it were. A spokeswoman for the reverend did say, however, that Ann has never been a "member" of Redeemer Presbyterian and that, while she may have attended services while in New York, none of the clergy at the church (including Keller) had ever met or interacted with her. The person I spoke to did not want to be named, but I got the feeling that she was less than thrilled that someone as bigoted and intolerant as Ann Coulter had associated herself with the church.

At the same time, whether or not Ann is a dutiful congregant at a particular house of worship seems to be beside the point. After all, "[r]eligious people have certain rules based on a book about faith with lots of witnesses to that faith."[23] Of course, that there are "lots of witnesses" to an idea could be said not only of the Bible, but of the Torah and the Koran, as well. Hell, even *The Social*

Contract. As we'll see in the chapter "Ann and Research," merely saying the other side of an argumentative divide is wrong doesn't make your side right. It's called the fallacy of negation, or the "either/or" fallacy, and it's one Ann falls victim to over and over again. Beyond that, the bigger danger lies in Ann's wielding of the Bible and her self-ordained sanctity. Hiding behind the rubric of religion, she contorts Christian doctrine to justify discrimination and her condescension toward those who don't conform. She's not flying planes into buildings in the name of Allah, but the contrast makes her hatred no less complete. Only those who haven't read what she's written or heard what she's said can believe her contention that all of her venom is just a joke. That it's all in the name of making her friends laugh. It's not. It's vile and virulent—and does far more to harm this country than it does to help it.

Chapter

Ann Has It Both Ways
OR
Mighty (Herm)aphrodite

> *There are substantive arguments contained
> in conservative name-calling.*
> —ANN COULTER, *Slander*

While logic and forthrightness are the tools of truth, their contrary counterparts—prevarication and hypocrisy—are the implements of last resort for those on the losing side of a discussion. Unfortunately, the latter often carry the day, especially when their source is someone seemingly in a position of authority. With her law degree, a handful of bestselling books, and countless opportunities to opine, Ann Coulter is one of these people. Add to that her knack for language and her understanding that copious citations lend credibility to a work, and it's a difficult war to wage against her. Which makes it all the more important that we do. Ann's authority is nothing more than a myth. She is the Wizard behind the Oz-ian curtain. But instead of awarding you the brain, heart, and courage you already have, she condones the bigotry, hatred, and contempt of those looking for an excuse to exercise them. And she will do whatever it takes, no matter how duplicitous.

Many of the recurring contradictions in Ann's arguments can be found with just minimal digging. A lot of them have been detailed so far—her hypocrisy about sex, her inconsistency on education, her simultaneous misogyny and batting of the eyelashes. What follows, then, are a number of Ann's efforts to both have and eat her rhetorical cake that don't fit neatly into the sections on the issues that she covers most often. That doesn't make them any less heinous. On the contrary, some of them are among the most flagrant of her fouls. And whether or not those scurrilous Web sites are onto something when they postulate that Ann was born with a penis and a vagina, her propensity to have it both ways seems a bit unfair. It is, indeed, a short trip to the land of Coulterian contradiction.

Among the most egregious examples is her repeated suggestion that criminals simply can't be rehabilitated. And what better way to prove it than to make a meal out of the twenty-year-old example of Willie Horton, the skeleton in Michael Dukakis's campaign closet. Horton, whose release from prison and ensuing crimes sent the former Massachusetts governor to the land of presidential also-rans, and to whom Ann devotes a whole chapter of *Godless*—in what could be seen as an inadvertent admission that she has nothing more recent to work with. In any case, it's Ann's stated belief that the best way to avoid recidivism "is to lock up all first-time criminals for life."[1] (Presumably, that includes George W. Bush for his 1976 DWI arrest and Rush Limbaugh for his repeated drug offenses.) But to be fair, a mandatory life sentence for jaywalking seems comparatively mild next to her "joking" suggestion that we deal with homosexuality as per Muslim Sharia law by dropping a wall on anyone found "guilty" of it.[2] (Presumably, *that* includes White House media suck-up Jeff Gannon and Dick Cheney's daughter, Mary.)

But back to the task at hand. Certainly Ann starts the day with every right to her belief that rehabilitation is an illusion. She may forfeit that right, however, when she regales us with the heartwarming tale of Brian Nichols.

Nichols, you may recall, went on a killing spree in March 2005 before winding up in the Duluth, Georgia, home of Ashley Smith (whom Ann obligingly refers to as "Christian" Ashley Smith). In wonderfully made-for-TV fashion, Smith purportedly began reading to Nichols from Rick Warren's sappily spiritual bestseller *The Purpose-Driven Life*. To make a long story short, Nichols "surrendered without incident, an utterly transformed human being."[3]

In an effort to better understand Ann's reasoning, let's break down her argument into its premises and conclusion:

First Premise: Criminals cannot be rehabilitated.
Second Premise: Brian Nichols is a criminal.
Conclusion: Brian Nichols was rehabilitated.

Okay—so Ann didn't actually say Nichols was "rehabilitated." And why would she? That would point to the success of some humanistic hard work. Rather, she says he was "transformed," by which she implies he was rehabilitated by the hand of God—and at the scene of the crime, no less! Yay, God!

———

In any event, you don't need to be a master logician to see the problem in this argument. Simply put, the conclusion does not follow the premises, assuming they're both true, which is undoubtedly a matter of debate, especially with regard to the first one. The only way for this argument to hold water is for us to assume that what Ann actually meant to say was criminals "cannot be rehabilitated . . . without divine intervention." Or in the case of Nichols, without the help of simplistic quasi-religious scribblings. In either case, maybe they should think about putting some Bibles in prison libraries or letting the inmates go to services or something. Really, they should do that.

———

Related to Ann's views on criminal justice is her obsessive devotion to the debunking of McCarthyism. In fact, much of 2003's *Treason* is a love letter to the man. According to the book's index, references to the Creator of the Cold War—the *roi* of the Red Scare, if you will—can be found on no fewer than eighty-eight pages. Ann uses much of that space to propagate the notion that McCarthyism "never existed."[4] As usual, it was all a liberal construct.

McCarthy was actually a beloved hero of the American people, Ann writes in the chapter "The Indispensable Joe McCarthy." Saying his "rhetoric was mild by the standards of the time." Much in the way, one imagines, she considers her own bile to be mild-tempered, the great man's errors were "infinitesimal compared to liberals' tearful testimonials to their own victimization."[5]

No comment.

So, fine—let's accept the premise that the sympathetic senator was just trying to help. He didn't mean no harm. And yet, if that's true, then why suggest that emulating the great man will give conservatives a leg up in their battle against liberals?

Speaking in February 2005 at the Conservative Political Action Conference, Ann suggested that conservatives take a page from McCarthy's handbook and persecute left-leaners the way the good senator sniffed out commie pinkos. At the conference, which *Time* called "the premier annual event for movement conservatives," Ann's speech was "part right-wing stand-up routine ... and part bloodcurdling agitprop."[6]

"Liberals like to scream and howl about McCarthyism," she told the conference. "I say, let's give them some. They've had intellectual terror on the campus for years ... It's time for a new McCarthyism."[7] Presumably, its having never existed won't pose a problem in finding a "new" one.

Whether or not McCarthy really was responsible for the Communist witch-hunts that defined much of postwar America, it's clear that he was adored and respected by the common man. He was "beloved by workers," he had "a gift for appealing to the great common sense of the American people," he was "a poet," "lots of Americans seemed to like him," he "had the hearts of the American workers," his was a "nonexistent crusade" (that word again!) that has "become a fact by sheer repetition." And, of course, the "public loved him."[8]

Interesting, then, that he died not just censured but "despised at forty-eight years old, his name a malediction."[9] It's tough to see how someone so cherished by the average American could have been so "despised" when he met his Maker. Then again, there have been one or two other historical figures who were persecuted despite performing their own brands of miracles. But awarding McCarthy some grade of messianism doesn't make the person doing so seem so sane. The next thing you know, Ann will be telling us "WWJD?" means "What Would Joe (McCarthy) Do?"

LATE-NIGHT LAUGHS

Like anyone who courts publicity the way Ann does, she's become a target of late-night comedians. Here's what the two biggest had to say:

David Letterman

— "Abu Musab al-Zarqawi was the world's most unhinged lunatic. He's dead now, so that moves Ann Coulter up to first place."

— "Al Gore has now produced a news documentary all about Ann Coulter. It's called 'An Inconvenient Bitch.'"

— "Here's what we know about Ann Coulter: She's blond, she's single. Maybe someone will set her up with O.J."

— "Anybody here from New Zealand? They have a big new attraction. It's a live sex show in New Zealand. They have actual bulls mounting a simulated cow. Good to see Ann Coulter getting some work."

Jay Leno

— "Secretary of Defense Rumsfeld said al-Zarqawi was 'mean, vicious and hateful.' So you know what that means. Ann Coulter could be next."

— "Ann Coulter is going to be on the show tomorrow night. Security is very tight. In fact, there is even restricted airspace over the studio. Her people are afraid that Dorothy's house could drop on her."

Ann saves some of her most insidious contradictions for Supreme Court justice Ruth Bader Ginsburg. Regarding Harry Blackmun's 1973 majority opinion in *Roe v. Wade*, Ann says that "[e]ven ... Ginsburg has called *Roe* an act of 'heavy-handed judicial intervention' and ridiculed the opinion during her confirmation hearings."[10] The implication that Ginsburg was or is in any way opposed to the ruling in *Roe v. Wade* is a true-to-form—i.e., really nasty—exaggeration on Ann's part. Far from "ridiculing" Blackmun's opinion, what Ginsburg did was question the basis for the decision—but *not the decision itself,* which she staunchly agreed with. As Pulitzer Prize–winning author Linda Greenhouse writes in *Becoming Justice Blackmun*: "In her scholarly way, Ginsburg had been a critic of *Roe*" but "not for its outcome, which she fully supported."[11] Hardly the sort of "ridicule" Ann alleges.

As if that wasn't enough, Ann later refers to Republican senators' confirmation of "extreme left-wing lawyers to the Supreme

Court, such as former ACLU lawyer Ruth Bader Ginsburg."[12] Let's take another look at a typical Ann argument:

First premise: All liberals care about is *Roe v. Wade*.
Second premise: Ruth Bader Ginsburg is a liberal.
Conclusion: Ruth Bader Ginsburg is against *Roe v. Wade*.

Even someone who wouldn't know a Venn diagram from an upskirt photo can spot the problem with this one. As Julian Baggini and Peter S. Fosl point out in *The Philosopher's Toolkit,* an argument can be said to be valid when "the conclusion is in some sense . . . presented as following from the premises *necessarily*" (emphasis theirs). "A valid deductive argument is one for which the conclusion follows the premises in that way."[13]

———

Another of Ann's favorite tricks is to use a particular source as the voice of authority (the *New York Times*, perhaps?) and then to ridicule others for doing the same. A really lovely example involves the use of college professors.

In her *Godless* effort to tear down the U.S. educational system—and, yes, blame it on liberals—Ann cites a study that "statistics professor Charol Shakeshaft"[14] did of a survey by the American Association of University Women Educational Foundation.

You get that so far? It's a study of a survey.

Onward, logician soldiers.

According to Ann, Shakeshaft estimated that "between 1991 and

2000, roughly 290,000 students were subjected to physical sexual abuse by teachers or other school personnel."

All righty. That seems eminently believable. Deplorable, but believable. And Ann actually offers attribution for the estimate. It seems only fair from a reader's perspective to assume that the citation refers to either the survey by the AAUWEF or to Professor Shakeshaft's study. Unfortunately, neither is the case.

In its entirety, Ann's endnote reads: Domingo Ramirez Jr., "Teacher Sex-Abuse Cases Soar," *Fort Worth Star-Telegram* (Texas), October 29, 2004. Which means that she couldn't be bothered to look up either Shakeshaft's study or the original survey. In other words, it's a secondary (or, possibly, tertiary) source—the use of which Ann herself despises, as you will soon learn in the chapter "Ann and Research."

Anyway, with curiosity now piqued, a closer look at the numbers is revealing. A total of 290,000 students over ten years (1991–2000, inclusive) comes to an average of 29,000 a year. Yes, that's an annual 29,000 too many, but suddenly what started out as a pretty alarming number seems ... well, not so much. Ann goes on to say that Shakeshaft has also determined, in a study for the U.S. Department of Education, that "about" one in ten kids has been sexually abused at school in some way. (Journalism tip number 372: pay close attention to the "abouts.") And this time, Ann cites the study itself.

The problem is that she doesn't tell you that in the preface to the 2004 study, U.S. Deputy Secretary of Education Eugene Hickok, a George W. Bush appointee, noted that Shakeshaft used "limited research" and that "the author's findings are broader than the congressional mandate and therefore could be perceived by some as insufficiently focused." Meanwhile, her use of the terms "sexual misconduct" and "sexual abuse" interchangeably (despite differences legal and otherwise) is "potentially confusing" and thus casts doubt on the findings.[15]

What Ann also doesn't tell you about the study is that kids were asked if anyone (students *or* teachers or other school employees) engaged in any of the items on a list of offenses when the respondents did not want them to. Included on the list is: "made sexual comments, jokes, gestures or looks."

On top of that, Shakeshaft's study found that "[o]f the students who experienced any kind of sexual misconduct in schools, 21 percent were targets of educators, while the remaining 79 percent were targets of other students."

Again, none of this is designed to defend unwanted sexual advances—especially when kids are involved. It is merely to point out that it is reprehensible of Ann to equate an undeniable instance of sexual abuse at the hands of a teacher with overhearing a dirty joke told by another student.

"The overwhelming majority of America's educators are true professionals doing what might be called the 'essential' work of democracy," Deputy Secretary Hickok wrote in the preface to the study. "The vast majority of schools in America are safe places."

Maybe it's no surprise that the math got a little fuzzy for a while there. After all, besides never telling us where Shakeshaft teaches—a quick Internet search shows her at Hofstra University in Hempstead (Long Island), New York—it turns out that Ann's description of Shakeshaft as a "statistics professor" falls outside the margin of error. It turns out Shakeshaft is a "researcher in the area of gender patterns in educational delivery and classroom interactions."[16] Which leads us to one of two possible conclusions: Ann's research was so shoddy as to allow such an error, or her description of Shakeshaft was intentionally misleading because "statistics professor" sounds a little more academically trustworthy than "researcher in the area of gender patterns in educational delivery and classroom interactions."

So here's the bottom line: even giving Shakeshaft the benefit of the doubt and accepting her estimate of 29,000 students who suffer sexual abuse each year, there are 55.3 million school-age kids in the United States. This figure comes according to a study by the National Center for Education Statistics of the Department of Education, which can be found at http://nces.ed.gov, and is for 1996—which means it's low. But that's okay because it'll work in Ann's favor.

Suddenly, that "about one in ten" that Ann seemed so intent on ramming down the reader's unwitting throat looks a lot more like just over 0.05 percent—also known as one in almost two thousand. Factor in Shakeshaft's admission that only about a fifth of those cases are at the hands of educators, and we're talking one in ten thousand. So, basically, the one in ten estimate was off by . . . let's see . . . carry the one . . . *a factor of a thousand.*

But, y'know—ballpark.

———

Which brings us full circle, to Ann's hypocritical use of a college professor as the voice of authority. Simply put, it's funny how things change. A short four years before, Ann saw fit to ridicule the *New York Times* for doing the same thing. (The *Times*, by the way, is cited in 20 percent of the endnotes for *Godless*, as you'll see in the chapter "Ann and Research.")

Ann, her words thick with contempt, writes on page 214 of the paperback version of her *Slander* that in "[a]ttempting its own definition of the religious right, the *New York Times* reported in 1986, 'Evangelical Christians are more easily led than other kinds of voters.' The *Times* cited a college professor as its authority."[17]

Of course, at least the Gray Lady cited a *religion* professor.

––––––––

Ann's contempt for the *New York Times* runs deep. That's no secret. Beyond her lament that Timothy McVeigh didn't target the paper's headquarters in Manhattan instead of the Alfred P. Murrah Federal Building in Oklahoma City, Ann has lately been calling for the execution of *Times* staff members for treason. In her July 12, 2006, column, she rehashes some of what she wrote three years earlier in *Treason*. As the story goes, then governor of California Ronald Reagan—who, it has been rumored, "won the Cold War"—told President Nixon in 1972 that Walter Cronkite and CBS News would have been charged with treason if their reporting about Vietnam had been similar during World War II.[18] Ann gives no indication of how Reagan's role as Professor Peter Boyd in 1951's *Bedtime for Bonzo* qualified him to comment authoritatively on such an issue.

Regurgitating references to Bill Clinton, McCarthy, and the Rosenbergs, Ann contends that the *Times* reports on the National Security Agency's eavesdropping are treasonous—or, as she said during a July 12, 2006, appearance on *The Jon Caldara Show* on KOA radio station in Denver, "something that could have gotten them executed."[19]

Okay, fine—so Ann thinks the *Times* building should be blown up, executive editor Bill Keller drawn and quartered, and staff members sent to perdition. She also joked to *Women's Wear Daily* that she was responsible for sending an envelope containing white powder (which turned out to be cornstarch) to the *Times* in mid-July.[20] What a laugh riot.

But what about the much-farther-right *Wall Street Journal*? Does sharing an ideology with its editorial page change the way Ann deals with the citadel of capitalist coverage? Well, it does and it doesn't.

When reminded by Caldara that the *Journal* had run similar stories, Ann played dumb, prefacing her judgment by saying she didn't "know the details of who printed what when." Which is a roundabout way of saying she would rather not bad-mouth a newspaper she actually likes. But as if realizing she had better stay on message, she then reluctantly conceded that she would "have no problem with prosecuting them for treason, either."[21] (Perhaps overlooking the fact that printing a news story about illegal surveillance by our own government may not actually *be* treasonous.) In what was then an inadvertent admission that her opinions were just a tad less than fully informed, Ann said, "[w]hatever the facts are, fine, but I'll let the prosecutors and the jury and the judge deal with that."[22]

Clearly uncomfortable, and reluctant to advocate the murder of *Journal* staffers and the destruction of its offices, Ann quickly fell back to her familiar flaying of the *Times*. "The point is we know what the *Times* is up to because they have a pattern of conduct here," she said.[23]

Setting aside the probable legal inadmissibility of Ann's perceived "pattern" of behavior, the point here is that sometimes refusing to have it both ways is as sneaky as doing so. And, worse, it's all so clearly premeditated. Using the most backward reasoning, Ann begins with the conclusion that the *New York Times* is evil and then casts around for premises to support it—to the absolute avoidance of any evidence. It's on par with the current administration's ever-shifting "justification" for the invasion of Iraq—Saddam Hussein was instrumental in the 9/11 attacks, he has weapons of mass destruction, he's an evil dictator who slaughters his own people, we need to spread democracy through the Middle East. Ann's retrofit rationalizations similarly throw her arguments into an unflattering light—with every wart and wrinkle accentuated.

Chapter 7

Ann on 9/11
OR
With Friends Like Ann, Who Needs Enemies?

For a fleeting moment, after the September 11 attack on America, all partisan wrangling stopped dead. The country was infused with patriotism and amazingly unified.
—ANN COULTER, *Slander, 2002*

I've never seen people enjoying their husbands' deaths so much.
—ANN COULTER, *Godless, 2006*

Unquestionably, September 11, 2001, has been the biggest-ever boon to the neoconservative movement. It assured George W. Bush a second term in office and has been used to justify nearly every action of the current administration—from immigration control to the government's illegal spying on its own citizens to the unprecedented and unprovoked invasion of another country. And, to our national disgrace, the driving force behind its success has been scare-mongering. The Republican machine has leveraged the residual fear we all feel to push through policies that in times of more-rational debate would be laughed at. A huge number of Americans have been scared into agreeing that we should give up some of our basic civil liberties in order to prevent another similar attack—even as one of the many justifications for invading Iraq is to spread the very freedoms we seem so keen to forfeit. The good news in all this is that a fair few of us seem to be catching on.

This does not bode well for Ann Coulter.

Much of the recent flap over her statements about 9/11 have centered on how she has dealt with the so-called Jersey Girls—four women who lost their husbands at the World Trade Center in New York. But insensitive comments like the one above from *Godless* have been flowing from Ann's mouth since . . . oh . . . September 12, 2001. Take this one: "We should invade their countries, kill their leaders and convert them to Christianity."[1] Of course, by "their countries," Ann seems to have meant "anywhere there are Muslims—except Saudi Arabia, because they pretend to like us and George Bush knows a bunch of people there." Even as recently as August 2005, Ann seems to be confused about who was responsible for the attacks on the Twin Towers and the Pentagon. "It's far preferable to fight [terrorists] in the streets of Baghdad than in the streets of New York (where the residents would immediately surrender)," she wrote in her column in August 2005.[2]

But the latest brouhaha may be the one that turns the tide on old Ann. Her criticism of the Jersey Girls has caused not just her usual detractors but those who formerly supported her to turn up their noses. And it's immaterial whether or not you think people like the "Witches of East Brunswick," as Ann calls them, have "absolute moral authority" because of their loss. The utter insensitivity of

Ann's comments is surely a contributing factor to the hate for her that floods the Internet and the focus on her writing that has fueled the charges of plagiarism.

"These broads are millionaires, lionized on TV and in articles about them, reveling in their status as celebrities and stalked by grief-arazzis. I've never seen people enjoying their husbands' deaths so much."[3]

Here's the thing, though: Suggesting that someone—Cindy Sheehan, a family member of a 9/11 victim—has capitalized on an unfortunate opportunity to make a political statement and that such a thing is wrong would carry a lot more weight if it didn't come from someone who used Paula Jones as a career-ladder rung, flips her blond tresses on TV while proclaiming that her looks give her license to say what others won't, and whines about ad hominem attacks while calling mourners "self-obsessed."[4]

The unmitigated gall of Ann's statements about the widows, and the subsequent uproar from camps on both sides of the political divide, may have landed her book-promoting opportunities on the *Today* show and a seat at Leno's right hand. But even Ann's apologists seem rather quick these days to pass off her poison as merely the parroting of other pundits. Foremost among them has been *NewsMax,* a magazine and Web site founded by journalist Christopher Ruddy, formerly of the *New York Post* and the leading conspiracy theorist in the Vincent Foster suicide case. *NewsMax*—little more than a monthly screed bashing liberalism and celebrity behavior—is published in West Palm Beach, Florida, just miles from Ann's primary residence. In its July 2006 issue, the magazine gleefully points out that *Wall Street Journal* columnist Dorothy Rabinowitz made the same point about the 9/11 widows more than two years ago.[5] In an article titled "NBC News Slanders Ann Coulter" (and teased on the cover with "Coulter Fights Back"), *NewsMax* accuses NBC's Brian Williams of preaching about the incident and extensively quotes Ann without any mention of whether the magazine tried to contact Williams or anyone at NBC.

Perhaps seeking safety in numbers, Ann told Leno during her appearance on *The Tonight Show* that others have blazed the trail of criticism leveled at the widows.

"[O]ther people have written acerbic little remarks about Democrats sending out victims," such as "these four women from New Jersey, making the exact same points Howard Dean could be making," she said. "But in this case, their husbands died . . . [so] we can't respond."

Rabinowitz does seem to have been the inspiration for much of what Ann says about the 9/11 widows (and Cindy Sheehan). And Ann's admission of this is pretty ironic given the current focus on her alleged pilfering of prose. It lends a certain validity to the allegation that Ann not only pinches actual passages from other sources but also that many of her ideas are borrowed.

In fact, as Ann's colleague in conservative colloquy Michelle Malkin pointed out in her column on June 7, 2006, Rabinowitz "had the definitive piece on the 9/11 widows two years ago." Which makes one wonder why Ann felt the need to rehash the material. Admittedly, though, Ann took Rabinowitz's argument a step further than the *Journal* likely would have allowed—even on its staunchly right-wing editorial pages. Instead of a simple criticism of the purported politicization of grief, Ann turned it into a personal attack.

Writing in the "Opinion Journal" on April 14, 2004, Rabinowitz condemned the widows for their role in bringing about the 9/11 Commission and their striving to use the media to get answers to their questions. In an anecdote about the testimony of then national security adviser Condoleezza Rice, Rabinowitz writes, "The hearing room that day had seen a substantial group of 9/11 families, similarly irate over the Jersey Girls and their accusations ... [b]ut these were not the 9/11 voices TV and newspaper editors were interested in. They had chosen to tell a different story—that of four intrepid New Jersey housewives who had, as one news report had it, brought an administration 'to its knees'—and that was, as far as they were concerned, the only story."

The irony that Rabinowitz is writing not just *in a newspaper*, but in the newspaper with the second-highest circulation in the United States, seems to be lost on her. Clearly, it wasn't "the only story." The fact that the thread was picked up by Ann Coulter—a columnist who, at the time of this writing, was syndicated in more than one hundred newspapers—also seems to sort of speak to that point. Meanwhile, Rabinowitz's belief that Americans outside the media might have been experiencing a bit of what she called "Jersey Girls Fatigue" seems a bit irrelevant, given current attitudes about government failures leading up to 9/11 and the subsequent response of taking over a country that had nothing to do with the attacks. On top of that, the outrage leveled at Rabinowitz's presumptive protégée, our Ann, and her heartless "enjoying their husbands' deaths" comment is more of an indication that people are suffering from Hysterical Conservative Polemicist Fatigue than anything else. One of the testaments to that, on a side note, is the stagnation of Bill O'Reilly's audience, contrasted with the increase in, and younger-skewing of, the viewership enjoyed by comparatively liberal talking heads such as Keith Olbermann at MSNBC.[6]

Even Leno suggested that Ann's overblown language might have been a hurdle to getting her point across. "[I]t seems to me," he told Ann, "the words you've used have overshadowed the point that you were trying to make—to the point where people are upset about you attacking the widows, they don't understand the point you were trying to make. And I think most people still don't understand the point you were trying to make."[7]

Clearly, Ann doesn't see it that way. She subscribes to the notion, summed up neatly by Oscar Wilde, that the only thing worse than being talked about is not being talked about. All publicity is good. Or, in her words, "[i]f you are not being called outrageous by liberals, you're not being outrageous enough."[8]

But it's not just liberals who are denouncing Ann. Even darlings of the right such as O'Reilly—and the *really* far right such as the Reverend Jerry Falwell—have distanced themselves from the extremist views she spouts.

On May 22, 2006, in what started out as a lament about the "double standard" that exists in the treatment of conservatives and liberals in the mainstream media, O'Reilly complained on his syndicated *The Radio Factor* (seemingly without irony) about the upcoming appearance of the Dixie Chicks on the cover of *Time* magazine. The spin(e)less one assured his listeners that "no far right person in this country" would score such a gig. Conveniently forgetting that our Ann had been on the cover a year earlier, Bill went on to say that he doesn't agree with "70 percent of what [Ann] says."[9]

"I think she takes something and runs with it to a degree, which is funny," O'Reilly said. "I see a twinkle in her eye and I'm wondering, 'Is Ann doing this for theater?' I don't know, I can't—I can't say." In describing her opinions as "bombastic," O'Reilly also suggested Ann and Dixie Chicks lead singer Natalie Maines should debate in Madison Square Garden, and called what the two women have said "rhetoric . . . in the extreme."[10]

It wasn't the first time, of course, that Ann and O'Reilly had tangled. On the August 5, 2005, broadcast of *The O'Reilly Factor* on Fox News, the two sparred over how the war in Iraq was progressing. The host mentioned in his lead-in that the network's own military analysts had said the effort was "not going well," and he pressed that point with his guest. After some initial barbs, O'Reilly raised the specter of Vietnam, calling perceptions of an American loss in Southeast Asia "the biggest myth in the world."

Ann, taking O'Reilly somewhat by surprise, it seemed, disagreed and contended that the United States actually *did* lose the Vietnam War. As expected, she then proceeded to blame a premature pullout brought on by propaganda from faithless liberals such as Walter Cronkite.[11] Despite O'Reilly's past suggestions that the United States might need to pull out of Iraq[12]—thus contradicting his own criticism of a "cut-and-run" policy purportedly espoused by gutless liberals—the two went on to agree that more troops might be needed, and that as long as the United States maintained a presence in Iraq, we would win the war.

But even in the weeks that followed, as O'Reilly defended Ann's point of view about criticism of the war and her right to respond to the 9/11 widows, he questioned her methods. Equating Ann's quibbles with the widows to his own tearing down of Cindy Sheehan, O'Reilly pushed the notion that it would be "smarter" to refrain from "personal attack" (apparently thinking that calling someone "dumb" and a "coward," as he did with Sheehan, is nothing personal).[13]

Since then, Ann seems to have lost patience with Fox's biggest star. Appearing on MSNBC's *Hardball with Chris Matthews* on July 14, 2006, Ann was questioned by Norah O'Donnell about the perceived cruelty of the comments about the 9/11 widows. The guest host got the inquisitive ball rolling by referring to O'Reilly, laughingly, as Ann's "soul mate."

Ann, with obligatory shaking of the head, eye rolls, and running of the fingers through the mane, responded by joking that O'Donnell was just "insulting" her. She went on to say, "I love Bill O'Reilly, but he's been viciously attacking me." [14]

But O'Reilly is not the only Fox employee questioning Ann's methods. In fact, others have crossed over into outright impugnment. Writing in his June 8, 2006, "Grrr!" column on foxnews.com, Mike Straka called out Ann on her use of the word "harpies" to describe the so-called Jersey Girls, and quoted Bugs Bunny in calling her a "maroon."

"Ugly is the only way I can describe what Coulter has written," Straka continued. "Now I understand why *Time* magazine put her on the cover last year and made her look like a praying mantis.

"Coulter's comments would be more understandable if they were off-the-cuff remarks on some television show," he went on. "But these abhorrent comments were written in a book. Books don't just hit the printing press as soon as authors submit them to a publisher. They are edited."[15]

NICKNAMES FOR ANN THAT CAN BE FOUND ON THE INTERNET

Cuckoo Coulter

Rush Limbette

Beltway Barbie

Mann Coulter

Coultergeist

Annie the Trannie

Ann C*ntler

Straka, of course, may not have been aware of Ann's contention that *Godless* was the "least-edited" of her books,[16] and he went on to say that the inflammatory language was likely intentional in an effort to drum up sales. Straka suggested that Ann "may have underestimated how sensitive even her own audience might be to such an ignorant rant."[17]

Meanwhile, those even further right on the political scale have made it clear that her tone may be something short of Christian. *Time* magazine—in the issue featuring Ann on the cover, naturally—quoted the Reverend Jerry Falwell as saying he was a fan of Ann's views but that "he probably won't use her on Sunday morning in . . . church because she is capable of getting a little aggressive."

Obviously, much of that aggression has been aimed at the 9/11 widows and their endorsement—some would say bringing about— of the 9/11 Commission and its subsequent report.

In her related effort to shoot down the report, Ann questions the independence of the panel, saying it consisted of "five members chosen by congressional Democrats, four members chosen by congressional Republicans, and the chairman chosen by President Bush"[18]—who, if memory serves, is a Republican. Again, maybe numbers aren't Ann's strong point, but according to the current laws of arithmetic, a commission consisting of five people appointed by Democrats and five people appointed by Republicans is about as bipartisan as it gets.

In any event, her real problem with the 9/11 Commission seems to be the picking of "gutless moderate Republicans" to battle the Democrats' "liberal attack dogs." This, she says, would be like "a commission on henhouse management with the Republicans carefully choosing well-credentialed hens and the Democrats sending in bloodthirsty foxes"[19]—a metaphor that is not only trite, but breaks down when you consider the incongruity of someone's being simultaneously "gutless" and "well-credentialed." And, as ever, Ann doesn't quite explain how any of this is the fault of liberals. If, indeed, the Republicans' appointees such as commission chairman Tom Kean were "gutless," I would tend to blame the Republicans who appointed them.

"The 9/11 Commission was a scam and a fraud, the sole purpose of which was to cover up the disasters of the Clinton administration and distract the nation's leaders during wartime," Ann says.[20] As if that were even remotely true. But do the fatuous statements end there? No.

Ann saves much of her bile for an attempt to dispute the importance of the infamous Presidential Daily Briefing of August 6, 2001—you know, the one titled "Bin Laden Determined to Strike in U.S."—that landed on George W. Bush's desk thirty-six days before the 9/11 terrorist attacks. Ann's efforts to dismiss the PDB as merely a "Cliff Notes history lesson on al Qaeda"[21] are inane enough. But her suggestion that the *New York Times* should print the entire PDB shows an utter misunderstanding of the way newspapers operate. Which is funny, given that, despite what she would have you believe, Ann Coulter *is a member of the media*. A very well-known member of the media, with a handful of bestsellers to her name. So, when she wonders "why the media has shied away from printing" the PDB,[22] one waits with bated breath for her to do exactly that. Now is her chance to show the world what it's been missing for the past five years!

Instead, all we get is a list of three handpicked "facts" culled from the briefing, followed by Ann's assertion that "[w]hile the PDB had a lot of old news about bin Laden, it didn't have much to say about his future plans."[23]

Not to nitpick, but the title—the *title*—of the briefing is "Bin Laden Determined to Strike in U.S."

Ann goes on to provide a partial transcript of Secretary of State (then national security adviser) Condoleezza Rice's testimony at the 9/11 Commission hearings. (Ann refers to it as an "interrogation.") Basically, it's page space about as well spent as a pair of "Separated at Birth" photos of Rice and Alfred E. Neuman. Nonetheless, she quotes Rice as saying the PDB "did not warn of attacks inside the United States. It was historical information, based on old reporting. There was no new threat information, and it did not, in fact, warn of any coming attacks inside the United States."

Let's forget for a moment Ann's disappointing failure to actually print the PDB in its entirety (after all, *Godless* contains far more space than your average *New York Times* edition—so, surely, there was room). Let's also set aside that in doing so she is thus guilty of the exact things she despises. Lastly, let's overlook the fact that bin Laden's boys—not Iraq—actually *did* attack us, thus proving the PDB to be ... oh, what's the word?... *extremely prescient*. Are we to actually believe that the whole PDB misunderstanding is titular? (Insert your own boob joke here.) Should we have read "Bin Laden Determined to Strike in U.S." to mean he wanted to attack us in the past? Seems to me that, given the current immutability of the space-time continuum, the PDB is *nothing but* a reference to "future plans."

The defense of Rice and the use of her wacky testimony is what people in the skepticism biz call an "overreliance on authorities." As Michael Shermer says in *Why People Believe Weird Things*, authorities "by virtue of their expertise in a field, may have a better chance of being right in that field, but correctness is certainly not guaranteed."[24] Given that Rice was clearly *incorrect* sort of makes it hard to see how she was right.

In any event, if use of the word "historical" is meant to mean "outdated," not only is it wrong (a reminder: bin Laden's men *did* attack us), but it makes Ann (and Condi) full of baloney. Ann herself says that there is information in the PDB from as late as 1999.[25] Forgive my ignorance of terrorist-cell time lines, but it seems to me that stuff from within the previous two years is pretty relevant when it comes to plots to activate sleeper-cell members, get them flight training, and have them hijack a handful of planes to fly into skyscrapers. In fact, Osama bin Laden reportedly met with Khalid Sheikh Mohammed in early 1999 to endorse Mohammed's idea to use planes as weapons.[26] Simply put, a plot such as the one carried out on September 11, 2001, takes a fair bit longer than slapping together a diatribe against four women who lost their husbands in the worst terrorist attack in this country's history.

Instead of saving her tirades for something of true consequence, Ann can't help but continue to blather about the 9/11 "harpies," as she calls them—going on to assert that their "shelf life is dwindling." Which sounds like more than a little bit of projection. Kristen Breitweiser was widowed six years ago at age thirty. Simple math puts her at almost a decade younger than Ann. Meanwhile, Patty Casazza, the only other of the four widows mentioned by name in *Godless* (too much trouble to look up the names of Lorie Van Auken and Mindy Kleinberg?), is in her midforties—hardly geriatric. And I'm guessing that neither one of them hides her age. Ann is about forty-five—or, at best, forty-two or forty-three, depending on which lie you believe.[27] Ann's suggestion that someone younger than she is might be near the end of her ability to attract men smacks of bitterness, especially in the context of her laments about her romantic life.

Ann also claims that "[o]ther weeping widows began issuing

rules about what could be done at Ground Zero," which she says is among the "contributing factors to the fact that it's been five years since the 9/11 attack and Ground Zero is still just a big empty plot."[28] Given that since the attacks, there has been a Republican mayor in what Ann calls "the most dynamic city in the world,"[29] one is left wondering how that's the fault of liberals.

Occasionally, Ann does have some good advice. In that category is her warning that when someone is "hysterical about something, but short on details, your antennae should go up."[30] In that light, let's take a critical look at a statement from page 2 of *Treason*.

"One year after Osama bin Laden staged a massive assault on America, a Democratic senator was praising bin Laden for his good work in building 'day care centers.'"[31]

Let's see . . . that's fairly hysterical, and there aren't really any details. You know, like the name of the senator or where the information comes from. And so at first blush, it seems to be yet another of Ann's unsupportable assertions. It's probably an exaggeration at best but seems unchallengeable because of its vagueness. So it was quite a surprise to find the incident spelled out a mere 251 pages later.

"Senator Patty Murray . . . told a group of schoolchildren that America needed to understand why Osama bin Laden was so popular and concluded that Osama was beloved because . . . 'he's been out in these countries for decades building schools, building roads, building infrastructure, building day care facilities, building health care facilities and people are extremely grateful.'"[32]

Without belaboring the point, it should be noted that according to Michael Swetnam, an adviser to the Senate Special Select Committee on Intelligence and co-author of a book on bin Laden, Murray's comments were "mostly on the mark," the Associated Press reported. Swetnam said that since 1988, bin Laden "has been on a mission to build schools, roads and homes for widows of those killed in the fight against the Soviets in Afghanistan."[33] Typically, building a bunch of stuff for people tends to get them on your side.

So, agreed that the statement about bin Laden is true? That like it or not, the guy has built up some goodwill among a certain group of people in the Middle East and elsewhere? Good. Let's continue, looking now at Ann's assertion that Murray has somehow heaped plaudits on Osama bin Laden.

With Ann's two statements this close together, it's pretty clear that she has overstated the case. While the intervening 251 pages of *Treason* may make that a little more difficult to see, Murray has no more "praised" the Al Qaeda leader than Dick Cheney "praised" his pal Harry Wittington with some birdshot to the thorax. In fact, Murray's alleged homage included calling bin Laden "an evil terrorist" responsible for the deaths of thousands of Americans.[34] According to the Associated Press story about the brouhaha caused by her comments, Murray spokesman Todd Webster said her comments to a class at a Vancouver high school "were intended to get the students to think about America's role in the world and why bin Laden is popular in many poor countries." (Sorry—it's too late to dispute that Osama bin Laden is popular among a certain, albeit not very nice, group of people. You already agreed otherwise.)

"This was not a dossier of the great works of Osama bin Laden. This is about, 'How do we secure a better and stronger future for this country?'" Webster said. "Do we close our doors and hunker down, or do we engage the rest of the world?"

But Ann, like most conservative pundits, doesn't believe in nuance. Murray's comments—or, more specifically, the misinterpretation of her comments—were soon all over the *Drudge Report* and gave Sean Hannity something new to froth about. It's a "sell the sizzle, not the steak" technique that Ann and her neocon cohorts use to great effect. But perhaps not as well as the old bait-and-switch that Ann seems to have mastered.

A perfect example comes toward the end of *Treason*. In what Ann calls a "race to the bottom in the idiotic things celebrities said"[35] about the Iraq war, singer Sheryl Crow, as a budding Buddhist might, spoke of the "karmic retributions" of killing innocent Iraqis. "She seemed not to understand that America going to war is the huge karmic retribution," Ann writes. "They killed three thousand Americans and now they're going to die."[36]

It's almost no wonder that, sadly, a significant number of Americans think Iraq had something to do with 9/11. People like Ann keep making the link. And it's not just that the link is tenuous—it's nonexistent. Nobody in Iraq had killed three thousand Americans—that is, until our troops arrived there and were "greeted as liberators" by being shot and blown up. But Ann, who must think carpe diem means "complain every day," seizes the opportunity to 1) bash a celebrity, 2) promote the idea that Saddam Hussein masterminded the 9/11 attacks, and 3) show how swaggering she is by reminding us that "they" are going to die. It's a tirade trifecta.

It would have been a qualm quartet if only Ann hadn't used up the old "Iraq had weapons of mass destruction" canard earlier in *Treason*. Not only does Ann seem ignorant of the fact that Iraq had none, but she implies that it was on the verge of having atomic weapons.

"With Iraq we had a chance to avoid a nuclear standoff with a totalitarian despot and avoid the insane stasis of Mutually Assured Destruction."[37] Oh, brother. A "nuclear standoff" is what we had with the then Soviet Union. It's what we may ultimately have with North Korea or Iran. Our "standoff" with Iraq was about on par with one between Mike Tyson and Macaulay Culkin. Which is to say, the latter's no saint, but everybody's betting on the big fella.

Ann's problems are compounded by the fact that she doesn't quite understand who is standing behind whom. An inability to see which of our allies actually *did* support the invasion of Iraq, combined with a blinding hatred of celebrities, can sometimes be an obstacle to rational argumentation.

While accusing liberals of being "picky about their admiration for Western Europe,"[38] Ann seems to forget that she consistently promulgates the idea that the British continue to believe that Saddam Hussein sought uranium from Africa. Yet she arbitrarily eschews the adjective "British" when it comes time to denounce a couple of entertainers. To Ann, "Gwynnie Paltrow and Madonna—with their European homes, European husbands and European accents—are demonstrating the same unblinking devotion to America's enemies that we have seen in the past."[39]

Let's clarify something here: Paltrow and Madonna are married to *Britons,* and live in the U.K. You know, the Western European country that *supported* the U.S. effort in Iraq. Equating Gwyneth Paltrow's maintenance of a home in London with sheltering Al Qaeda operatives is no more accurate than saying Ann Coulter supports Fidel Castro because she lives in South Florida. While the U.K. may be part of Europe, it is only so by the technicality of geog-

raphy. There's a reason people call living in London "Europe 101"—
it has very little in common with living on the continent.

———

In any case, opposition to the Iraq operation must surely be con-
fined to the entertainment industry. A sweeping majority of Americans must support the war—which, incidentally, seems to have
ended three years ago when President Bush declared "Mission
Accomplished." All these polls and statistics showing otherwise are
just a sign of the media's liberal bias. It's probably a fair guess that
to know how Ann sees it, you can just substitute the word "Iraq"
for "Vietnam" in the following sentence from *Treason*: "Despite the
left's relentless effort to dishearten the nation, vast majorities of
Americans consistently supported the Vietnam War. The myth that
an anti-war movement swept the nation is preposterous."[40]

Now, insisting that McCarthyism "never existed"[41] is so roundly
absurd that it can be dismissed pretty much out of hand. But to
promote the idea that the protests and demonstrations against U.S.
involvement in Vietnam are mythical is too much to excuse.

There's no question that, as with Iraq, the administration boasted
strong early support for the effort—and with only slightly less
"serial" fabrication (in this case, the potential for a "domino effect"
of rampant communism). But over time, as casualties and expenses
mounted, and as it seemed that a favorable result was becoming
less and less likely, Ann's "vast majorities" dwindled. In early 1968,
support for the Vietnam effort slipped to a minority in Americans
aged thirty to forty-nine. They were soon followed by people under
thirty (who, contrary to conventional wisdom, had been most sup-

portive throughout). By May 1971, *opposition* to the war reached between 66 and 77 percent[42] for all age groups.

Of course, support for the invasion of Iraq was fairly strong back in March of 2003 when Ann trumpeted in her column that thousands of Iraqi soldiers had been captured and killed (no mention of the civilians who wound up likewise). At the time, she points out, "American forces [had] suffered fewer than two dozen deaths."[43] As of July 28, 2006, the number of American military casualties had grown to more than one hundred times that—to 2,569.[44] In fact, as you read this, there's a fairly good chance the number of American soldiers killed in Iraq will have exceeded the number of people who died in the 9/11 attacks. And that's not an "I told you so." It's a simple fact.

But, to borrow a militaristic phrase, Ann has stuck to her guns. In November of 2003, just six months after President Bush's "Mission Accomplished" flub, she pulled the old anti-Hollywood hammer from her tool belt, writing that "war is not as predictable as, say, a George Clooney movie."[45] Ann later wrote, in June 2004 (about eight months *after* the White House lied to distance itself from the fracas over the banner) that the invasion of Iraq "has gone fabulously well."[46]

And whether or not the *New York Times* has been "itching to use the word 'quagmire'"[47] since the start of the war, they aren't the only ones using it now. With more and more Republicans and other conservatives among them, it sort of lends the idea a certain legitimacy.

It's a standard conservative ploy to criticize those who draw parallels between the war in Iraq and Vietnam. But the fact is it's a lot more relevant to equate Iraq and Vietnam than it is to link Iraq and Al Qaeda. Take this entry on Vietnam from *Timelines of World History*: U.S. efforts "were undermined by the inability of its forces to come to terms with guerilla warfare and by the hostility of U.S. popular opinion to the war. By 1973, the U.S. was forced into a face-saving withdrawal."[48]

Will anyone be surprised to see that, for the Iraq reference in the 2010 update of the book, the editors have just cut-and-pasted that passage (à la our Annie) and changed the date? More interesting, perhaps, will be how the publishers handle the reason for the war in the first place. An "imminent threat" from Saddam and his tremendous stockpile of weapons of mass destruction? A filial grudge? An American thirst for oil so unslakable that even George Bush, a Texas oilman, suggested that we do what we can to cut back?

It seems that Ann would likely approve of the last one in that list. Relying on her go-to gizmo—the celebrity bludgeon—she promoted the crude idea that we *should* invade other countries and kill innocent people to make sure ExxonMobil Corp. makes another $10 billion in profit next fiscal quarter.

"Why not go to war just for oil?" she asks. "We need oil. What do Hollywood celebrities imagine fuels their private jets? How do they think their cocaine is delivered to them?"[49]

Funny line, sure. Maybe even enough to excuse the venom behind it. Or not. The fact is, a joke at a celebrity's expense is usually fine—many of them deserve it. Besides, we've all seemed to agree that that's the price you pay in this country for being in the public eye. But whatever leeway Ann is given to cut down a public figure should be questioned when the joke is so utterly tasteless.

This not to argue that her right to make the joke should be revoked. No—despite Ann's not being a big fan of the First Amendment, she is more than free to blather on, green-eyed, about the "beautiful people." But let's not lose sight of our right to tune her out. If conservatives are allowed to discount everything Bill Clinton ever said because he lied about Monica Lewinsky, if John Kerry can't be trusted because he "voted for the war before [he] voted against it," if Al Gore is to be considered a serial liar because he gave his wife a hammy kiss onstage, then we can in good conscience discredit any of Ann's blather about 9/11.

Ann's "stay the course" vision is more than just the rote conservative response to criticism that the war in Iraq was ill conceived and has been poorly executed. It is yet another of her habitual hardline stances to, well, everything. It is inflexibility in the extreme, and a reflection of her inability to consider an opinion other than her own. We all want to be right in our thinking, but most people would rather see the truth and base their ideas on it. Ann Coulter, on the other hand, is more concerned with feeding the ogre of her career—and the word "ogre" is not chosen haphazardly. In folklore, ogres are depicted as huge, hideous creatures that feed on human flesh. In more than one sense, that describes Ann Coulter's profession to a tittle. She is exploitative to a disturbing degree, with a success that is based on little more than the ability to make controversial and outrageous comments. She is more than happy to cannibalize her conservative cohorts to advance her cause and seemingly ecstatic at the prospect of brute personal attacks on those to the left of her.

Chapter

Ann and Research
OR
When the Cat's Away, the Mice Will Plagiarize

Most of what I say, I say to amuse myself and amuse my friends. I don't spend a lot of time thinking about anything beyond that.
—ANN COULTER in *Time*

I believe everything I say.
—ANN COULTER on *The Big Idea with Donnie Deutsch*

In June of 2006, in the weeks after the publication of *Godless* and just as the book began its rise to the top of the *New York Times* bestseller list, a number of liberal Web logs started to question the integrity of Ann's writing. More specifically, they began to accuse her of outright plagiarism. Some of the charges seem a little specious, pointing to passages that contain a handful of consecutive words that match another work or use similar language. But as the scrutiny began to intensify, it became pretty clear that larger and larger—if not necessarily significant—chunks of prose had been lifted from other sources and altered minimally, if at all.

Blogs such as The Rude Pundit and gawker.com were among those that kick-started the latest round of the plagiarism hunt. But such questions apparently go back quite a way. As reported by gawker.com, *Boston Globe* columnist Alex Beam in 2001 examined passages in *High Crimes and Misdemeanors,* Ann's first book, published in 1998. In an article headlined "High 'Crimes' and Misuse?" Beam "compared Coulter's prose to that of Michael Chapman, a former colleague of Coulter's who, in 1997, wrote 'A Case for Impeachment' in the popular right-wing nutjob periodical *Human Events,"* as gawker.com put it. The following passages were cited as examples of similar language:

Chapman: "Four Democratic fundraisers have stated that former DNC Finance Chairman Marvin Rosen explicitly advocated selling access to the President. . . ."

Coulter: "At least four Democratic fund-raising officials have revealed that former DNC Finance Chairman Marvin Rosen explicitly advocated selling access to the president. . . ."

and

Chapman: "A DNC fundraiser told Nynex executives they would receive invitations to White House 'coffees' if they joined the DNC's 'Managing Trustees' program and agreed to donate $100,000. . . ."

Coulter: "A DNC fundraiser told Nynex Corporation executives that they would receive invitations to White House coffees if they joined the DNC's 'Managing Trustees' program and agreed to donate $100,000. . . ."[1]

The *Globe* reported that Chapman had offered to ghostwrite *High Crimes*, and that at the time, Ann referred all questions to her lawyer, Richard Signorelli. "Ms. Coulter's book was not ghostwritten at all," the *Globe* reports Mr. Signorelli as saying. "Ms. Coulter researched and wrote the entire book from beginning to end with no assistance whatsoever from any ghostwriter." Signorelli reportedly added that Ann "does not even know who Mr. Chapman is." Given that Ann and Chapman were colleagues at the weekly *Human Events,* that denial seems about as plausible as Dick Cheney's saying he had never met John Edwards. Which is to say, Ann's response appears to be a bald-faced lie.

At the same time, the *Globe* reported that Harry Crocker, executive editor at Regnery Publishing—which published *High Crimes* and is owned by the same company as *Human Events*—said that a writer by the name of David Wagner had cobbled together information for a draft of the impeachment book.

"Ann read those chapters and she read Chapman's work as well," Crocker told the *Globe*. "They offered some basis for source material, but it was my impression that she threw those drafts away as irrelevant."

Pretty circuitous, yes—so here's the bottom line: a couple of dudes do some research for a book about the impeachment of President Clinton. One of them publishes an article based on the research. The other one starts a draft of a book. Ann reads the article (and—why not?—she works there) as well as the draft of the book. She decides, according to the publisher, that what she has read is irrelevant, and writes the book herself. Oddly, a number of passages from the article appear in her book virtually verbatim. She then, through her lawyer, says she doesn't even know the guy who wrote the article.

Which makes it all the curiouser for Ann to say that "[w]hen you write for a small-circulation newspaper like *Human Events,* your columns are apparently considered community property by other journalists, who shamelessly poach your work without the briefest little credit."[2] The wonderful phrase "hoist on one's own petard" comes readily to mind.

Now, whether all this is mere sloppiness or outright plagiarism is difficult to say. Even the second, longer example has passages that are only twenty-seven and twenty-nine words long, respectively. Hard to make such a serious accusation based on a couple dozen words. At the same time, there are those, such as the folks at gawker. com, who think such things will "do more damage to her reputation than any vile, inaccurate invective she's been spewing for the last seven years. The media will tolerate brutally meretricious bullshit, but God forbid you rip off another writer."[3]

———

Meanwhile, just a few days before the gawker.com piece, The Rude Pundit said Ann has a "bad habit" in that she "appears to like to copy whole sentences from other sources without putting them in as quotes or even citing where she might have 'paraphrased' from."[4]

The appropriately named Rude Pundit served up more-recent examples, including the following from Ann's latest book:

Ann in *Godless*: The massive Dickey-Lincoln Dam, a $227 million hydroelectric project proposed on upper St. John River in Maine, was halted by the discovery of the Furbish lousewort, a plant previously believed to be extinct.

The *Portland Press Herald*, in its 2000 list of the "Maine Stories of the Century": The massive Dickey-Lincoln Dam, a $227 million hydroelectric project proposed on upper St. John River, is halted by the discovery of the Furbish lousewort, a plant believed to be extinct.[5]

Not just slightly longer, but even closer to verbatim. Still, The Rude Pundit hesitated to call it plagiarism, while also "not saying it's not."[6] In any event, the site asks, "How harshly would Coulter judge a liberal writer for doing the same? Or would she have to be silent?"[7]

————

Still, these are blogs, after all. They appear on a new mass-communications service you may have heard of called "The Internet." As such, they surely can't be e-trusted as far as you can e-throw them, right? How about a mainstream—albeit tabloid—newspaper?

In the days after gawker.com and The Rude Pundit began their assaults on Ann, the *New York Post* picked up the thread, going so far as to hire a guy by the name of John Barrie—a professor and creator of program that detects plagiarism—to look at Ann's work. Those *bastards*. In a July 2, 2006, article by Philip Recchia headlined "Copycatty Coulter Pilfers Prose: Pro," the *Post* claims that Ann "cribbed liberally" in *Godless*. The paper cited Barrie, the chief executive officer of iParadigms, who used the company's iThenticate program to find at least three examples of "textbook plagiarism" in the bestseller.[8] While the *Post* also said Barrie discovered lifted passages in some of Ann's columns, the newspaper played up his pointing to a "25-word passage from the *Godless* chapter titled 'The Holiest Sacrament: Abortion' [that] appears to have been lifted nearly word for word from Planned Parenthood literature published at least 18 months before" *Godless* hit bookstores. The newspaper also said a "24-word string from the chapter 'The Creation Myth' appeared about a year earlier in the San Francisco Chronicle with just one word change," and that "[a]nother 33-word passage that appears five pages into *Godless* allegedly comes from a 1999 article in the *Portland* (Maine) *Press Herald*."

The charges of plagiarism seemed to come to a head in the first week of July, when the *Post* reported that Universal Press Syndicate, which handles the syndication of Ann's columns in more than a hundred newspapers, said it would probe the issue. In an article headlined "Coulter on the Carpet" by *Post* correspondent Niles Lathem, the newspaper quoted spokeswoman Kathie Kerr as saying that Universal takes "allegations of plagiarism seriously. It's something we'd like to investigate further."

But in the days following the investigation, Universal Press disputed the assertion that Ann had stolen any of her rapier-sharp prose. "There are only so many ways you can rewrite a fact, and minimal matching text is not plagiarism," syndicate President Lee Salem said in a statement. Universal Press "is confident in the ability of Ms. Coulter, an attorney and media target, to know when to make attribution." (Before calling a premature end to the witch-hunt, Salem may want to have a peek at Ann's Clarence Thomas–*New York Times* citation, detailed in "Ann on Beauty, Race, and Culture." To say Ann knows "when to make attribution" is a matter of some debate.)

While not actually denying any of the charges of plagiarism, Ann did respond in a column on her Web site by saying that the *Post*, "[o]nce considered a legitimate daily . . . has been reduced to tabloid status best known for Page Six's breathless accounts of Paris Hilton's latest ruttings, and headlines like 'Vampire Teen—H.S. Girl Is Out for Blood.' How crappy a newspaper is the *Post*? Let me put it this way: It's New York's second-crappiest paper." She went on to speculate that the *Post*'s "harassment . . . is an attempt to shake me down for protection money. . . . I have sold a LOT of books—more books, come to think of it, than any writers at the *New York Post*." Not to nitpick, but if the "I sold lots of books" defense was legitimate, James Frey would still have an open invitation to appear on *Oprah*.

NewsMax, meanwhile—in only the most impartial way, of course—said the "latest media attack on Ann Coulter seems to be a desperate measure to undermine the credibility of one of America's most prominent conservative voices."[9]

At the same time, *Godless* publisher Crown Publishing issued a statement from Senior Vice President Steve Ross echoing that Ann "knows when attribution is appropriate." The statement said the charges of plagiarism are "as trivial and meritless as they are irresponsible," and highlighted the book's nineteen pages of endnotes.

Godless does, in fact, have nineteen pages of endnotes. On those nineteen pages, there are 344 endnotes—which, frankly, pales in comparison to the 780 notes in *Slander,* as mentioned by Al Franken in his book *Lies and the Lying Liars Who Tell Them.* Franken also points out that endnotes are "harder to reference" than footnotes,[10] which appear at the bottom of the page that contains the cited material. In any case, many of them are vague or misleading enough as to be completely devoid of meaning.

Now, whether the inequality in the number of endnotes means readers should consider *Godless* to be only half as trustworthy as *Slander* is an open question. Both books have severely illusory citations and attributions. Additionally, of the 344 endnotes in *Godless,* at least 70 of them—more than a fifth—come from the *New York Times*, and at least two of the notes reference multiple *Times* articles. Which is interesting, given Ann's rather unflattering opinion of the Paper of Record.[11]

For someone who repeatedly accuses the *Times* of outright fabrications, she cribs an awful lot from it. And not in the way I'm doing here with her books. Time and time again, Ann uses the *Times* as an authoritative source. Meanwhile, Ann's beloved *Wall Street Journal* is worthy of just a few citations in *Godless.* In fact, despite the seemingly huge overlap in ideology with the *Journal*'s opinion pages, Ann doesn't have much nice to say about the paper.

In *Godless,* Ann calls *Journal* science reporter Sharon Begley an "ignoramus" for allegedly accusing "critics of evolution of having small minds for refusing to believe" in the theory.[12] As yet another of the aforementioned ad hominem type of attack, this also contributes to Ann's ongoing "fallacy of negation," which basically involves the attempt to discredit one position in the effort to make one's own "correct." As Shermer points out in *Why People Believe Weird Things,* it is a "favorite tactic of creationists," who "spend the majority of their time discrediting the theory of evolution so that they can argue that since evolution is wrong, creationism must be right."[13]

Of course, Ann also (wrongly) accuses Begley of succumbing to something she calls the "argument from the counterintuitive." But as often happens when reading *Godless,* we're being misdirected. The point here is that Ann is all for the *Journal* when it's bashing Bill Clinton, singing the praises of tax cuts for the rich, and supporting military involvement in Iraq. But that unconditional puppy love becomes ambivalence at the first sign of equivocation from the *Journal.* Even a hint of dissent, the merest suggestion that the paper might not toe the party line, is punished.

In a section of *Treason* crediting Ronald Reagan for the dissolution of the Soviet Union (like *that* wasn't gonna happen anyway), Ann is outraged that the *Journal* would have "criticized Reagan for making 'a bad deal' and subjecting our European allies to Soviet intimidations."[14]

After all, Reagan "won the Cold War," he "defeated the Soviet Union," he "prevail[ed] over an evil empire to win a half-century war with the USSR," he won "a final victory over Soviet totalitarianism," he was responsible for the "annihilation of the Soviet

Union," he "won the Cold War," he "won the Cold War" (for a third time), he "vanquished the evil empire," he "won the Cold War," he stopped the Soviet Union "dead in its tracks!" (exclamation point hers!), he was responsible for the "transformation of Cold War tactics," he "waged the Cold War with relish," he "spent six years bleeding the Soviet Union from every limb," his "victory over the evil empire was complete," he "consigned the USSR to the dustbin of history," he "forever destroyed the Soviet war machine," he, yes, "won the Cold War," he "won the Cold War," he "vanquished the Soviet Union," he "won the Cold War," he "won the Cold War," he "won the Cold War," he "won the Cold War," he "won the Cold War," he "won the Cold War."[15]

So, wait—Ronald Reagan did what now?

———

Anyway, back to business: The endnote accompanying her criticism of the *Journal* is actually a citation from a 1987 article by Stephen Chapman called "Zero Option Evokes Zero Honesty in Some Conservatives" from the *Chicago Tribune*. In other words, she's quoting the *Trib* quoting the *Journal*.

In yet *other* words, it's material from a secondary source. Which isn't a crime and probably wouldn't be noteworthy if Ann hadn't flipped her dye job about eighty pages earlier about the use of secondhand sourcing. "Flip through any book on McCarthy and notice the footnotes. It is an arresting fact that the supporting documentation rarely consists of primary source material,"[16] she writes.

But even projecting this purported villainy onto others while engaging in it oneself could be forgiven if it was rare. Unfortunately for Ann, it's apparently a jones she still needs to feed. Instances pop up fairly often in *Godless,* including her "quoting" from Darwin's *The Origin of Species* through the book *Icons of Evolution* by Jonathan Wells.[17] Another involves a completely specious reference to criminal justice in which she cites an October 1993 editorial in the *Augusta Chronicle* citing the *Wall Street Journal.* Finally, because things come in threes, she quotes Truman-era judge David L. Bazelon and his ideas about imprisonment, but does so from a book called *Vision of the Anointed* by Thomas Sowell. Not exactly the "primary source material" she so values.

Sadly, it's pretty much a given that by the eighth or ninth time your cat pees on the living room rug, you tend to become inured to it. Sure, it's still not pleasant, but at that point all you can do is shake your head and clean it up. Page after page of unsupported assertion and rancor in Ann's books similarly desensitizes the reader. Instead of gagging, as the reader might through the first half of *Godless,* we start to laugh at her incorrigibility.

"[Y]ou let a lot of it go, even when her views tend towards the obnoxious and her journalistic methods towards the pretty appalling," the *Guardian* wrote. "It's not just the factual slips—she cites Bobby Kennedy's assassin, Sirhan Sirhan, as an early example of Islamic terrorism, even though he was a Christian—but her willingness to make the most sweeping, generalised statements on the flimsiest of evidence. Of course, this is an occupational hazard in the opinion business, but Coulter is still an exceptional case."[18]

Is this to equate Ann's writing with cat pee in the same way her opponents are accused of equating Iraq to Vietnam? You be the judge. Comparisons aside, such hubbub can be better prevented.

It's probably no stretch to say that Ann's next book (suggested working title: *Jobless—How to Cut-and-Paste Your Way to Ignominy*) and her columns are going to receive a little more editorial scrutiny than she has enjoyed thus far. Like, of the extreme variety.

By Ann's account, *Godless* was the "least-edited" of her books, with just "a few changes here and there. But not much," she told Jay Leno. Instead, she apparently has her drinking buddies check her punctuation and spelling. "I had a lot of my friends read the book before it came out," she said. "I gave it to my smartest liberal friends. . . . And I said, I want you to attack this book. You go through it with a fine-toothed comb."[19]

As much as that makes for decent talk-show banter, it's doesn't really meet the standards of journalistic integrity that Ann tends to demand from the mainstream media. But, okay, Ann doesn't work for the *New York Times*. *Godless* is a book—and a polemical one at that. There's room for opinions, assertions, allegations, and blather. *Godless* shouldn't be viewed as journalism any more than Donald Rumsfeld should be seen as a huggable teddy bear. It's not news. But neither was that midterm paper sophomore year—the one when you got busted for copying out of *Funk & Wagnalls* and making up half the bibliography. Coincidentally, Ann's faux pas are "the same sort of things that would flunk an English 1A student, you know, writing some term paper on the same type of subjects," Barrie told Keith Olbermann about the verbatim passages.

"This is not Ann Coulter . . . these are works from third parties that were used without citation," Barrie went on, explaining that his company examined *Godless* and some of Ann's columns at the *Post's* request. "We found multiple examples of this sort of thing. . . . After a while we just gave up—we said, 'look, there's enough of it, there you go. You know, we're done reading Ann Coulter's work.'"

Of her attributions, Barrie said it was "extremely unclear what the citations were referring to. She had citations, maybe three or four paragraphs later—but, you know, the preceding four paragraphs were all quoted from the same source. So, you know, it was that sort of free and loose use of citations that made it very, very difficult to try to determine whether Ann Coulter was citing that material or whether she was just trying to pass it off as her own."

Meanwhile, *Human Events* editor Terence Jeffrey defended his biggest star in a CNN report on July 7, 2006. Regarding the alleged theft from Planned Parenthood literature, he asked, "Does anyone really think that Ann Coulter is trying to plagiarize Planned Parenthood? Ann is not a reporter, she's a commentator. She takes her facts from other sources."[20]

Anecdotal evidence suggests it was all Jeffrey could do to refrain from using air-quotes (" ") around the word "facts."

———

Regardless, to say that someone with a column syndicated in more than one hundred newspapers and who has written for countless magazines and periodicals "is not a reporter" is true only in the most Coulterian sense. Which is to say, by the slimmest technicality. Granted, she doesn't cover breaking stories, attend White House press conferences, or compile box scores for Florida Marlins games. But by virtue of writing about current events for *newspapers,* she is a *journalist,* and is thus beholden to the same standards of *journal-*

ism that she so forcefully reminds us exist for the likes of *New York Times* columnist Maureen Dowd or former CBS anchor Dan Rather. (And, whether she wants to admit it or not, she is governed by a far higher standard of truth, accuracy, and attribution than is Michael Moore, the conservatives' favorite punching bag.)

Contrary to a long list of Apologists for Ann, John Dean doesn't seem willing to give her the benefit of the doubt. In *Conservatives Without Conscience*, Dean lumps Ann in with other conservative authors who have made a living out of trashing liberals, and he questions her legitimacy as a trustworthy source.

"Take the 'queen of mean,'" he says. "*Slander*, for example, contains page after page of scorn, criticism, belittlement, and bemoaning of ideas she believes liberal. Her books have also generated a subsidiary cottage trade in fact-checking her work, which has amply demonstrated that Coulter apparently considers accuracy as something that needs only to be approximated."[21]

This sort of in-the-ballpark accuracy should not be seen as an accident or the result of laziness. Ann Coulter is too intelligent and too ambitious for it to be so. The exaggerations, red-herring citations, and masterful misdirections are executed with the utmost intent. Every last one of them. It's no stretch to say that Ann relies on her readers' quick trust of "authority" and their desire to agree with someone who articulates their deepest prejudices—not to mention the predisposition of all of us to figure that a footnote must be nothing more than some Latin abbreviation and reference to a page number that bears out what was just said and doesn't need to be flipped to, much less questioned. She uses our societal attention deficit disorder to her advantage—speaking and writing in the sort of convenient sound bites that get her air time on *Today,* ink in the *Times,* and notoriety nonpareil. These are tactics ripped right from the neoconservative playbook. Mislead, redirect, and reduce to a blurb. It's time we played more defense.

Chapter

Ann Speaks

OR

Under a Series of Men
Is Not the Only Place She Lies

*When arguments are premised on lies,
there is no foundation for debate.*

*Arguments by demonization rather than
truth and light can be presumed
to be fraudulent.*
—Ann Coulter, *Slander*

One of the conservatives' biggest battle plans involves the promotion of creationism as an alternative to the teaching of Darwin's theory of evolution. This is, of course, yet another wedge to drive down the middle of the political spectrum in an effort to mobilize the religious segment of the right, irrespective of whether it's a viable plan. When even the pope, in this case John Paul II, says that religious doctrine leaves room for the truth of evolution, the leg that so-called intelligent design stands on gets pretty arthritic.

And that's putting it kindly. The fact is, the denial of evolution as the pre-eminent explanation for our existence is tantamount to an outright lie from the likes of Ann Coulter. There is simply no way that her refutation of the overwhelming evidence in favor of evolution is anything but a political stance. That said, such fabrication is certainly her right.

Despite Ann's baseless assertion that liberals are "enraged that Republicans are allowed to talk back,"[1] instances such as allowing the neo-Nazis to March in Skokie, Illinois, might lead you to believe otherwise. In fact, most Americans would probably vehemently defend Ann Coulter's right to say just about whatever she wants. But understand that when the first premise in a book is an outright lie, a reader has the right—nay, the obligation—to question, discount, and largely disbelieve everything that follows.

————

In the spirit of this, let's take a look at page 1, paragraph one of *Godless*:

> Liberals love to boast that they are not "religious," which is what one would expect to hear from the state-sanctioned religion. Of course liberalism is a religion. It has its own cosmology, its own miracles, its own beliefs in the supernatural, its own churches, its own high priests, its own saints, its own total worldview, and its own explanation of the existence of the universe. In other words, liberalism contains all the attributes of what is generally known as "religion."

Even granting that more than just about none of that is true, Ann ought to stop buying her dictionaries on the discount rack. In the entry for "religion" in my Webster's unabridged there is no mention of the words "cosmology," "miracle," "church(es)," "priests" (high or otherwise), "saints," "worldview," or "universe." As a kindness, let's give her "supernatural" because it does make reference to that which is "beyond the visible world." What it does say is that religion "operates through faith or intuition rather than reason."[2] Not much of a leap, then, to say that religious zealots such as La Coulter are, by definition, unreasonable.

But, see, we're already off track. This is what Ann does—she makes statements so ridiculous on their face that it's easy to get caught up refuting the minutiae instead of pointing out that she's just told a big fat lie. By her standards, *baseball* is more of a religion than liberalism (just ask any Red Sox fan).

Ann also repeatedly (and erroneously) ascribes religiosity to those who have the audacity to think evolution might be even remotely on target. She truthfully—if irrelevantly—points out that "before Darwin, the accepted explanation for the chain of life was design."[3] Yes, and before Copernicus, the accepted explanation for dawn and dusk was that the sun revolved around the earth. And Ann wonders why people who agree with the principles of evolution reckon that those who aren't so discriminating are all members of the Flat Earth Society. (Web site: www.alaska.net/~clund/e_djublonskopf/Flatearthsociety.htm)

Simply pointing out that a belief existed before science came along with a vastly superior explanation is not an argument to disbelieve the science. On the contrary, it's fair enough to say that one of the more important Socratic notions decreed in the *Dialogues of Plato* is the demand that, when presented with two opposing arguments, the laws of philosophy and truth seeking demand that one believes the stronger of the two.

Okay, fine—maybe the *Dialogues* stuff is a little outdated at 2,400 years old. Let's move forward a couple millennia to Scottish philosopher David Hume, who published the seminal philosophical treatise *An Enquiry Concerning Human Understanding* just a score of years before our Founding Fathers were dashing off what Ridgemont High's Jeff Spicoli rightfully refers to as the "cool rules" of our Constitution. Hume, doing more for rational thought than Angelina Jolie does for heterosexual males—and a fair few females, for that matter—synthesized the aforementioned Socratic notion better than anyone before or since.

"[N]o testimony is sufficient to establish a miracle unless the testimony be of such a kind that its falsehood would be more miraculous than the fact which it endeavors to establish . . . I weigh the one miracle against the other . . . and always reject the greater miracle."[4]

In other words, it makes sense to reject the outlandish claim that in a mere six days an unseen divine force created all the flotsam of the universe—including our own Big Blue marble and all its inhabitants—in favor of a theory that has a century and a half of hard science in support of it. It is not merely preferable to do so; it is your duty as a thinking human being.

Ann's contention that evolution is "about one notch above Scientology in scientific rigor"[5] is what psychologists call "projection"—the ascribing of characteristics (especially those that are undesirable) to another. When Ann calls Darwinism a "make-believe story, based on a theory that is a tautology, with no proof in the scientist's laboratory,"[6] she violates the skeptic's guideline that scientific language does not make science[7] (note her use of the word "tautology") as well as erroneously transferring the burden of proof back onto evolutionary theorists. Not only did Darwin base his theory on actual empirical evidence, but the intervening 150 years have seen the collection of mountains of clues and the formulation of demonstrable scenarios based on those clues. As a result, evolutionists faced with the charge that they have no evidence in their favor can hardly be blamed for their "I'm rubber, you're glue" response.

The fact remains that at this point in our collective scientific understanding, it is "up to creationists to show why the theory of evolution is wrong and why creationism is right, and it is not up to evolutionists to defend evolution," Shermer writes in *Why People Believe Weird Things*.[8]

But it's hard to expect much from someone who, again erroneously, claims that those who pitch their tents in the evolution camp consider Darwinism to be a "fact."[9] In *fact*, scientists, educators, and other evolution supporters are very careful *not* to call evolution a "fact," and just as careful to refrain from calling creationism a "theory." (Take a closer look at the above passage from Michael Shermer, for example.) A theory is, properly, a "more or less verified or established explanation accounting for known facts or phenomena."[10] Darwinism (evolution) is a theory. A hypothesis, meanwhile, is "conjecture put forth as a possible explanation of certain phenomena."[11] Creationism is a hypothesis—and a pretty bad one at that, if the complete lack of supporting evidence is any measure. And slapping the euphemistic tag "intelligent design" on it doesn't make it any less so.

To be fair, the misunderstanding may come from the tendency of us all to use the word "theory" in its colloquial sense—as in, *I have a theory about why Ann Coulter is so sniffish*. A theory isn't just a guess, a hunch, or a sneaking suspicion. It's a conclusion based on identifiable and attestable premises. As Tim M. Berra, professor of zoology at Ohio State University at Mansfield, puts it in his book *Evolution and the Myth of Creationism*, when tests "repeatedly confirm" a hypothesis, it results in the "erection of a theory." Furthermore, no theory, "even evolution, is ever held to be sacred; but some are more durable than others, as near to unchallengeable as makes little difference." Pretty diplomatic stuff.

But let's assume that Ann, despite being a product of the public school system—you know, where American children "fall behind [foreign kids] with each additional year"[12]—learned enough at the Ivy League's Cornell University to differentiate between a scientific term and a colloquialism. What she clearly does not understand is evolution theory itself. With regard to the emergence of new species, it is Ann's idea that "[i]n order to get to the final product, each one of the hundreds of mutations needed to create a functional wing or ear would itself have to make the mutant animal more fit, otherwise it wouldn't survive" and that the "vast majority of mutations are deleterious to the organism."[13] This demonstrates a profound misunderstanding of natural selection. It's on par with saying that a woman born with an excessively protuberant Adam's apple is thus doomed to spinsterhood and, consequently, the extinction of her bloodline. (Hmm . . . maybe this isn't the best example.)

The bottom line is that a mutation may have no immediate effect on the "fitness" of the organism—or at least no effect detrimental enough to ensure its extinction. Yet the organism may pass this new characteristic on to future generations until it combines with other mutations to the degree that a new species is born. Yes, this may take *billions* of years. But hey, we can't all get things done in under a week.

If Ann had read *The Origin of Species*, she would know, also, that the term "survival of the fittest" doesn't appear anywhere in the text. The term was actually coined by biologist Herbert Spencer (who, incidentally, formulated his ideas about evolution before Darwin did and, in fact, popularized the term "evolution"). In any event, it's an oversimplification—to the point of being flat-out wrong—of Darwinian theory. It's the "Play it again, Sam" of evolutionary science.[14] So, one of two things could have happened here: 1) Ann has never read *The Origin of Species,* and therefore shouldn't be commenting authoritatively on it, or 2) Ann has read Darwin and is therefore being disingenuous or, to be kind, forgetful.

———

Like many proponents of creationism, Ann goes on and on about the intricacy of things like the human eye, DNA, and flagellum. Such things are so complex, she asserts, that we must assume they are the work of a creator. Even Darwin "noted the difficulty of explaining the eye in *The Origin of Species,* admitting he could not do it," Ann writes.[15] Disappointingly, she does *not* then point out that, similarly, ancient Egyptians couldn't explain why the sun came up every morning—therefore we must assume a hawk-headed man-god named Ra was responsible.

Of course Darwin couldn't explain the eye—he was doing his research during the Victorian era, for Pete's sake. You know, when "state of the art" was, like, one of those creepy metal clamp thingies that can only be found in museums or Nine Inch Nails videos. Not exactly high-powered software. Which, incidentally, Ann claims has so far also failed evolutionists.[16] But hey, it took Wilbur and Orville a couple tries. They didn't fly the first time. Should we then not believe that airplanes can get off the ground? Do you suppose Ann takes Amtrak when she travels between her Manhattan pied-à-terre and her Palm Beach lair? Let's break down her argument to its component parts, as we did to such great effect earlier.

> **First premise:** Scientists can't explain the complexity
>   of the eye.
> **Second premise:** *There ain't one.*
> **Conclusion:** Ann doesn't believe in airplanes.

That's just a bit of silliness, of course. The "real" conclusion to her argument is: *We must assume a creator.* But when evaluating the soundness of the reasoning, both the joke conclusion and her actual one are equally farcical.

The problems with Ann's reasoning are legion. In this case, not only is her conclusion drawn from a single premise—a philosophical no-no known as *induction*—but it suffers from the false notion that "unexplained" equals "inexplicable." Or, as Shermer, a professor in the cultural studies program at Occidental College in Los Angeles, puts it in *Why People Believe Weird Things,* there are "many genuine unsolved mysteries in the universe, and it is okay to say,

'We do not yet know but someday perhaps we will.'"[17] Problems arise, he writes, because "[m]ost of us . . . want to control our environment, and want nice, neat simple explanations. All this may have some evolutionary basis." (Oh, the irony.) But "in a multifarious society with complex problems, these characteristics can . . . interfere with critical thinking."[18]

Instead of engaging in her own critical thinking, Ann is content to bolster her argument with a previously detailed flaw in her reasoning—the overreliance on authorities. In this case, it's her use of Bill Gates and his thoughts about DNA—the double-helix structure of which Francis Crick and James Watson didn't discover until about a century after *The Origin of Species* was published, by the way. She quotes Gates as saying that DNA is "like a computer program, but far, far more advanced than any software we've ever created."[19] Recent reports that Microsoft's operating system has no fewer than twenty-one "vulnerabilities"[20] might cause one to rethink the use of the world's richest man as the arbiter in *Evolution v. Creationism*. Better, perhaps, to use . . . oh . . . say, *National Geographic*, whose staff might know a thing or two about anthropology. In the magazine's assessment, the dismissal of evolution as "just a theory" is about as good an idea as disbelieving that your toaster will brown your bread if you plug it in and use it properly. After all, "even electricity is a theoretical construct, involving electrons, which are tiny units of charged mass that no one has ever seen."[21]

Similarly, Ann might also want to steer clear of relying on Cambridge astrophysicist Fred Hoyle. According to Hoyle and his colleague Chandra Wickramasinghe—both of whom, Ann hastens to point out, were atheists—the odds that life could have arisen by random processes are so minuscule as to "make Darwin's theory of evolution absurd."[22] Of course, Hoyle and Wickramasinghe had "no expertise in biology or paleontology, do not understand natural selection, and have espoused a variety of anti-evolutionary ideas."[23] Among their wacky notions is "panspermia," which is the idea that life spread to Earth from infectious agents that came to us on comets. No kidding. How life could have started elsewhere—but certainly not here—isn't addressed. And kudos to Ann for calling the idea a "little nutty." Points deducted, however, for writing that "unlike evolution, 'panspermia' has the virtue of not being demonstrably false."[24]

In any case, Ann ought to be done with Hoyle. And, by name, she is. But along with promulgating the idea that we are, essentially, aliens (one of the hazards of spending your workday looking at the heavens), Hoyle had a bogeyman in the form of the archaeopteryx. This feathered birdlike dinosaur, dating back to the Jurassic period about 150 million years ago, gave scientists their most famous transitional fossil[25]—i.e., one that shares the characteristics of two taxonomic groups, or what we laypeople call a "missing link." In this case it's the link between reptiles and birds. Hoyle and Wickramasinghe claimed that the first archaeopteryx fossil, discovered in Germany, was in part a forgery. That's *their* problem. Ann's problem, on the other hand, is joining them on the anti-archaeopteryx bandwagon.

Just a single page after reminding *Godless* readers of the incompleteness (she says "paucity") of the fossil record and asking why it doesn't show "*any* bad mutations"[26] (emphasis hers), she contradictorily calls archaeopteryx "just an odd creation that came out of nowhere and went nowhere."[27]

Also going nowhere is Ann's effort to highlight a supposed rift between evolution scientists who espouse gradualism—the idea that changes occur very slowly—and those who embrace punctuated equilibrium—in which changes happen in fits and starts. Her contention that the latter (who, it should be noted, remain in the minority) have merely tried to make evolution consistent with the fossil record[28] is . . . well, there's not really a word for it. To say that some scientists have modified their theory because of new evidence is true. It also happens to be *exactly what scientists are supposed to do*. That's what differentiates them from the blindly faithful.

But perhaps the most important difference between evolutionists and creationists—and it's one entirely ignored in *Godless*—is their respective relationships to their literature. Even allowing the conservative canard that "intelligent design" is a scientific theory, it is a theory based on "authoritative" writings, which are held up as the evidence. Whereas with evolution, the writings—*The Origin of Species* et al.—are based on the evidence, which informs the theory. Without getting too esoteric and philosophical, suffice it to say that evolution theory meets the standards of the scientific method. Meanwhile, "creation science" is merely the contention that the Bible is true because it says so in the Bible. That's what philosophers and logicians—and other people who, albeit insane, are far smarter than most of us—call "begging the question."

The point of all this is not to suggest that creationists are wrong, but rather to detail the flaws in Ann's ability to reason—a list that is legion and bleeds into other of her opinions.

In a July 2001 column on the now-defunct watchdog Web site Spinsanity (www.spinsanity.org), cofounder Brendan Nyhan does a brilliant job of dissecting Ann's arguments and highlighting how she uses emotive words and false analogies[29] to mask the inadequacy of her reasoning.

In "Ann Coulter: the Jargon Vanguard," Nyhan points out that Ann's columns "often open with inflammatory attacks like calling Ted Kennedy an 'adulterous drunk' and joking that President Clinton had 'crack pipes on the White House Christmas tree.'" Nyhan goes on to say that "[o]n a more sophisticated level, Coulter's writing is full of the sweeping generalizations attacking liberals that are the stock in trade of many conservative pundits. These arguments take a particular case (often presented in a distorted way) and use it to attack all liberals, erasing any some/all distinction."

And that was before 9/11.

"Another tactic," Nyhan argues, "is simply associating liberals with lists of code words: the Democratic message is 'socialism, class warfare and atheism'; liberalism is 'the official government religion' and is 'devoted to class warfare, ethnic hatred and intolerance'; 'God has no part in the religion (liberalism) of sex education, environmentalism, feminism, Marxism and loving Big Brother.' Coulter seems to be unaware of the irony in her statement that 'name-calling has been the principal argument liberals have deployed against conservative arguments.'"

And Ann is certainly not unaware that a belief in God cuts across party lines. A Harris Poll in October 2003 showed that while only 36 percent of Americans attended a religious service at least once a month, almost 80 percent of respondents professed a belief in

God.[30] Democrats just aren't as willing to jump on the biblical band-wagon to make a political point as Republicans are.

But opportunistic or not, four bestsellers and counting is a pretty strong argument that Ann Coulter is a decent writer, whether you agree with her politics or not. She can turn a phrase with the best of them, and, perhaps most importantly, knows how to cover her rear end—legally speaking, anyway. Ann is masterfully magnilo-quent, a purveyor of parenthetical red herrings, the doyenne of the dependent-clause disclaimer.

But the Spinsanity boys were onto her.

Quoting from a column in which Ann says Democrats on the Senate Judiciary Committee repeatedly accused "John Ashcroft of essentially belonging to the Klan and harboring a secret desire to take away women's right to vote," Nyhan points out the "tremen-dous amount of emotional, loaded language jammed into that dependent clause. In fact, no one accused Ashcroft of belonging to the Ku Klux Klan, let alone repeatedly (note the weasel word 'essen-tially')."[31]

Which seems like, and is, a rather astute deconstruction of her inflammatory, overblown claim. But it's tough dealing with the mistress of misdirection. Ann's absurd contention about the KKK accusation draws all the reader's attention, leaving the second part of it, Ashcroft's being accused of "harboring a secret desire to take away women's right to vote," to float through uncontested—even though it's equally spurious. If we can forget for a second that while Ann implies that an antisuffragette viewpoint would be a bad thing, she herself has said that women shouldn't be allowed to vote. And it's pretty clear that the addition of a second component to the

Ashcroft phrase is linguistically deft. Insidious, to be sure, but absolutely brilliant.

And it's a monkey wrench she pulls from the tool chest again and again, to varying degrees of success. Sometimes, this sort of second-condition component can turn what would otherwise be an outright lie into a statement that, while true enough, is misleading at best. When Ann writes that the United States is "the only modern democracy founded on the belief that all men are created equal; the only modern democracy that fought a revolution to redeem that idea and a civil war to prove it,"[32] it's true as far as it goes—i.e., about as far as Rush Limbaugh after three Vicodin and a fifth of Jim Beam.

After all, these days Francophobia may be de rigueur, but let's not forget that the unwashed masses of Paris were no less revolutionary and democracy-demanding than American colonials. Just ask Louis XVI, who, just a few short years after the storming of the Bastille, was removed from his head. In fact, the only thing that makes Ann's statement even technically true is that the French weren't stupid enough to need a civil war to end the enchainment and forced servitude of other human beings. (One point for the Gauls.) But again, at the risk of getting all Noam Chomsky on you, Ann is nimble enough to structure the sentence so that the punch comes from the "all men are created equal; the only modern democracy that fought a revolution to redeem that idea" part. (Which, if you'll pardon the long digression, actually isn't true at all. And not just because the Founding Fathers owned slaves and didn't let the womenfolk cast ballots, but because of the way our voting system is set up. In the wake of the 2000 presidential election, we all heard more than we cared to about the Electoral College and how archaic it is. But the fact remains that we don't have the one-person, one-vote kind of democracy that exists in countries like . . . oh, let's pick one at random . . . say . . . France.)

And if it weren't enough to lord over our Western European comrades the American distinction of having killed hundreds of thousands of ourselves in order to preserve the union, she goes on to say we're "the only modern democracy that nearly single-handedly smashed Hitler's Germany and Stalin's Russia."[33]

Yeah. Right.

Forget the half million or more British soldiers killed during World War II—after all, there were no "Support the Troops" magnets stuck to the rears of Morris Minors back then, so they really don't count.

Now, if that's a swipe at France for having rolled over when the Germans marched into Paris, fine. Though let's not forget that our bailing them out in World War II merely balanced out the ledger, considering that without French help, we'd all likely be eating bangers and mash paid for in pounds and pence. But if you're going to eat Freedom fries and boycott Bordeaux wines, then spare us the hypocrisy of using France as an example . . . well . . . of anything.

In a diatribe (entirely without attribution—or merit) about how liberals are standing in the way of progress in U.S. energy policy, Ann writes that "in a spasm of left-wing insanity in the seventies, nuclear power was curtailed in this country."[34] She continues by saying that "Japan has nuclear power, France has nuclear power—almost all modern countries have nuclear power."

Well, *so do we.*

Skipping right past her revelation that around the time of the Three Mile Island disaster, concerns about the dangers of radioactive waste moved our leaders to become a little wary of atomic power. Or, as she puts it, "we had Jane Fonda in the movie *The China Syndrome.*"[35] Either way, the implication that France generates nuclear power and we don't is not only false but also hypocritical.

And Ann has the cojones to say that "liberals are very picky about their admiration for Western Europe."[36]

Yeesh.

———

Similar to the "evident" accusation that John Ashcroft is a Klansman is a statement about Ann's good friend Matt Drudge, who is "evidently accused of extracting semen from Bill Clinton and placing it on Monica Lewinksy's dress."[37]

Now, leaving out the ridiculousness of such a thing, it's difficult to see why Ann wants to invoke any kind of sympathy for Drudge (who, you'll recall, inadvertently kicked Ann under the bus by spilling the beans on the size of her book advances). Still, there it is— her defense of him, at the end of a list of purported "liberal media bias" offenses. Which may make the Drudge reference the most insidious and effective of them all. You see, it comes after Ann contends that "Rush Limbaugh has been blamed for the Oklahoma City bombing," that the "editorial page of the *Wall Street Journal* was accused of driving Vince Foster to suicide," and that "Fox News is charged with plotting to steal a national election."[38] As marginally truthful (which is to say, not at all) as those three things may be, they seem infinitely more so next to the ludicrous reference to Drudge.

Sometimes, it's not what you say, but what you don't say, that makes you a discreditable alarmist. Take a look at the following passage (emphasis and footnotes added) from the hardcover edition of *Slander:*

> The day after seven-time NASCAR Winston Cup champion Dale Earnhardt died in a race at the Daytona 500, almost every newspaper in America carried the story on the front page. Stock-car racing had been the nation's fastest-growing sport for a decade, and NASCAR the second-most-watched sport behind the NFL. More Americans recognize the name Dale Earnhardt than, say, Maureen Dowd. (Manhattan liberals are dumbly blinking at that last sentence.) **It took *The New York Times* two days to deem Earnhardt's death sufficiently important to mention it on the first page.** Demonstrating the left's renowned populist touch, the article began, "His death brought a silence to the Wal-Mart." The *Times* went on to report that in vast swaths of the country people watch stock-car racing. Tacky people were mourning Dale Earnhardt all over the South!

It's probably not much of a stretch to say you noticed the bold-faced type. And who can blame you if you believed that the *Times* completely ignored the tragic death of one of the most popular race-car drivers in the country? After all, the *Times* "regularly interprets standard Republican positions as fanatical,"[39] while their journalists "create a smokescreen for the liberal monolith."[40] On top of that, the paper "has transformed into a caricature of the old reactionary WASP establishment, swatting down the social-climbing middle class with their polo mallets."[41] Given the clear allegation of classism, it seems pretty easy to believe not only the general assertion that the *Times* is a liberal rag that ignores anything outside of the New York metropolitan area (and, moreover, anything enjoyed by non–New Yorkers), not to mention the specific allegation that it would pass on a story about the demise of a leading figure in a sport generally seen as catering to hicks and other rubes. Is there any impugning this "fact"? Well, it seems there is.

Simply put, Ann's statement that the *Times* was anything but prompt in reporting Earnhardt's death is a complete fabrication. A distortion. A *lie*. But it gets even worse—it soon became an *exposed* lie. Which makes it all the more insufferable, particularly for someone who has built a career on prevarication and the eyelash-batting talent to pull it off. As Al Franken points out in *Lies and the Lying Liars Who Tell Them*, the day after Earnhardt's horrific accident, "the *Times* ran a front-page account of Earnhardt's death written by sportswriter Robert Lipsyte under the headline: 'Stock Car Star Killed on Last Lap of Daytona 500.'"[42]

Okay, so Ann got busted. She told a lie, and someone—well, not just someone, but her nemesis—called her on it. Surely, being the self-aggrandizing truth seeker that she is, she will rectify the situation.

Guess again.

Check out the passage from the paperback edition of *Slander:*

The day after seven-time NASCAR Winston Cup champion Dale Earnhardt died in a race at the Daytona 500, almost every newspaper in America carried the story on the front page. Stock-car racing had been the nation's fastest-growing sport for a decade, and NASCAR the second-most-watched sport behind the NFL. More Americans recognize the name Dale Earnhardt than, say, Maureen Dowd. (Manhattan liberals are dumbly blinking at that last sentence.) Demonstrating the left's renowned populist touch, the article began, "His death brought a silence to the Wal-Mart." The *Times* went on to report that in vast swaths of the country people watch stock-car racing. Tacky people were mourning Dale Earnhardt all over the South![43]

Note the conspicuous absence of the line about the *Times*'s alleged crime against circular driving. A simple typographical error? Oh, no. An oversight? Uh-uh. A contemptible, cowardly, deceitful, devious, furtive, low (sound of flipping thesaurus page), shifty, slippery, underhanded way to get out of admitting you lied? You be the judge. And bear in mind that there's no mention, anywhere in *Slander,* of the removal of the line. No room, even for a 781st endnote.

Now, say what you want about the *New York Times*, but excising an error in the hopes that no one will notice is not exactly its modus operandi. To wit: executive editor Howell Raines's falling on his sword in the wake of the Jayson Blair scandal.

For those of you who have just returned from a decade living out of radio range in the Australian Outback, Blair was the *Times* reporter who, it was discovered in 2003, had faked quotes and interviews, plagiarized from other newspapers, and submitted false expense records to deceive the paper about his whereabouts.

One suspects that if Ann Coulter had been in charge of all the news that's fit to print, she would have pretended as if the Jayson Blair incident had never happened. Maybe she would have stolen out under cover of the night to burn all extant copies of the paper with Blair's stories in them. Or perhaps just flipped her overprocessed hair in an effort to mesmerize the American public so that it wouldn't know what had gone on.

The *Times*? Well, it admitted to thirty-six instances of journalistic fraud by Blair, ran a series of front-page corrections detailing every possible error, and called the incident "a low point in the 152-year history of the newspaper." Joining Raines, managing editor Gerald Boyd resigned about a month after the scandal, and the paper had soon created the position of public editor, whose evaluations of the *Times*'s reporters, techniques, and culture are published every two weeks.

Talk about sweeping it under the carpet. Seriously—what a bunch of sneaky cowards those guys are at the *Times*.

Still, maybe Ann deserves some slack. After all, she did remove the error so that generations of neocons can enjoy her perspicacious prose in perpetuity without danger of thinking the *Times* had done anything untoward. Or will they?

Setting aside the fact that removal of just that one line left the passage with a complete non sequitur for the unwitting reader to decipher, what is left still implies that the *Times* is so out of touch with "mainstream" America that its "article began, 'His death brought a silence to the Wal-Mart.'" But, see, that was an article written two days later. The first sentence of the *Times* piece the day after Earnhardt went to that big two-and-a-half-mile oval in the sky was: "Stock car racing's greatest star, Dale Earnhardt, was killed today as he tried to block a car from catching the two front-runners on the last turn of the sport's premiere event, the Daytona 500."[44]

It's pretty clear from the paper's description of the Daytona 500 as the "sport's premiere event" and their reference to Earnhardt as its "greatest star" that someone at the paper with the country's third-highest circulation has at least a clue about NASCAR. Hell, they even spelled his name right.

In an e-mail response to *Time* magazine's John Cloud, Ann repeated the lie that the article began with the Wal-Mart reference. As Cloud reported, Ann responded by writing, "I think I can save you some time. . . . The one error liberals have produced is that I was wrong when I said the [*Times*] didn't mention Dale Earnhardt's death on the front page the day after his death. There have been novels and Broadway plays written about Ann Coulter's one mistake, which was pretty minor . . . the *Times* article DID begin: 'His death brought a silence to the Wal-Mart.'"[45]

But, again, as Cloud points out: "Actually, it didn't. . . .The article doesn't mention Wal-Mart, although a subsequent piece did."[46]

And so we're left with Ann Coulter's self-described "one error."

––––––––

Whether Ann has made just this one mistake or many, it may be time for the rest of us to take a piece of her advice. Think back to her suggestion that the best way to avoid repeated criminal behavior is to imprison offenders for life. We need to throw Ann Coulter into the jail of oblivion and irrelevance. Without the opportunity for parole. And we need to do so as soon as possible.

The reality, of course, is that it's too late to stop Ann at just a single crime against reasonable debate. After all, she has five books on the shelves, has seen hundreds of her columns make it to print, and appears on national television dozens of times a year—all of which means her rap sheet of rhetoric contains offenses numbering in the thousands. And her crimes are nothing less than heinous. Ann's harangues, her name-calling, and her outright lies are the felonies of discourse that have divided this country. And no matter how much she may backtrack, they are *not* simple crimes of passion—not instances of temporary insanity, forgivable because they were carried out in the heat of the moment. No, Ann Coulter's contributions to political polarization are premeditated to an obscene degree. They are meticulously thought out, executed with verve, and, unfortunately, usually have the desired effects: promotion of the neocon agenda and making Ann more money.

It's time that Americans with an interest in our country took a stand and started to see through the static clouding an otherwise clear view of its future. We should banish Ann Coulter and those like her (right and left) from our otherwise rational national dialogue. No more buying her books, no more reading her columns, and no more paying her to poison our students' minds. Whatever usefulness she may once have had has run its course. Ann Coulter adds *nothing* to our exchange of ideas but an ugly weight that drags it further into the colloquial quicksand.

This is not to demand conversational civility at the expense of the truth. Rather it is to demand the truth at the expense of selling books. If the *New York Times* is guilty of treason, gather the evidence and present it in a clear and concise way. If embryonic-stem-cell research really isn't so hot, point us to the facts and figures that prove it. If the war in Iraq is something we should support, substantiate your view. And if you'd like, be passionate when you do so. You can even be funny if you want. Just don't misdirect us to make a point. Don't stoop to vindictive personal attacks to distract us from the matter at hand. And whatever you do, don't lie to strengthen your case.

The danger in our metaphorically revoking Ann's privileges is that it must come in stages—and will likely result in her increased desperation to be heard and all that that entails: fouler rancor, nastier "jokes," and ever-filthier lies. It will be near impossible to simply shut off the spigot of Ann's sludge. These things don't happen overnight. She is no doubt right now sifting through invitations to speak on college campuses while her agent negotiates the advance on her next book. And with an election imminent, she'll certainly get her mug on cable television with increasing regularity. The time has come to change the channel.

Acknowledgments

There are any number of friends and family to whom I owe whatever success this book may find. Among them are my parents, for their encouragement and willingness to engage in the sorts of conversations that lend themselves to sociopolitical awareness; my sisters and nephew, for making me laugh when I'm being too serious; Pud Tinkler, for the same; Lynn Grady, for bringing my idea to life, and Mauro DiPreta, for shaping it so deftly; the Lovely Girl, for her inspiration; Richie Fox and Vince Vecchio, for keeping me grounded; the Daisy-Pattons, for always being there; the fellas, for making my formative years so entertaining; Chris Gatto, my first editor, for making me care about language; V-Rod, for all the help; Michael Shermer, for so clearly articulating what's wrong with conventional "wisdom"; and Ann Coulter, for being such an easy target.

Notes

Chapter 1

WHY ANN COULTER MUST BE STOPPED

OR

"ANNOYANCE" STARTS WITH "ANN"

1. Richard H. Davis, "The Anatomy of a Smear Campaign," *Boston Globe*, March 21, 2004.

2. Ann Coulter, *Slander—Liberal Lies About the American Right* (New York: Three Rivers Press, 2002), p. 13.

3. Ibid., p. 22.

4. Ann Coulter, *Godless—The Church of Liberalism* (New York: Crown Forum, 2006), p. 103.

5. Ibid., p. 112.

6. John Cloud, "Ms. Right," *Time*, April 25, 2005.

7. Ibid.

8. Coulter, *Slander*, p. 26.

9. Ann Coulter, *Treason—Liberal Treachery from the Cold War to the War on Terrorism* (New York: Three Rivers Press, 2003), p. 15.

10. In a poll of "greatest ex-presidents," on Web site The Cellar (cellar.org), Carter garnered 44.4 percent of the vote, four times the tally of Theodore Roosevelt, Calvin Coolidge, Gerald Ford, and Bill Clinton—all of whom tied with 11.1 percent. Of course, there were only eighteen voters, and it should be noted that neither Ronald Reagan nor George H. W. Bush were among the choices.

11. Coulter, *Slander,* p. 260.

12. Coulter, *Treason,* p. 12.

13. Nielsen BookScan, as of the week ending July 9, 2006.

14. Video of the exchange can be seen on the Media Matters for America Web site at http://mediamatters.org/items/200410160003.

15. Coulter, *Slander,* pp. 3–4.

16. This refers to the title of Chapter 5 of *Godless,* "Liberals' Doctrine of Infallibility: Sobbing Hysterical Women."

Chapter 2

ANN ON BEAUTY, RACE, AND CULTURE

OR

THE POT CALLS THE KETTLE THE "NEW BLACK"

1. U.S. Census Bureau (www.census.gov). The number represents the three-year average for 2000–02.

2. Ibid.

3. Coulter, *Slander,* p. 35.

4. Ibid.

5. Cloud, "Ms. Right," *Time.*

6. Coulter, *Slander,* p. 41.

7. Andrew Gelman, Boris Shor, Joseph Bafumi, David Park, "Rich State, Poor State, Red State, Blue State: What's the Matter with Connecticut?," November 2005. (A report about the study can be found on the

Washington University of St. Louis Web site at http://news-info.wustl.
edu/tips/page/normal/6885.html.)

8. Ann Coulter, *How to Talk to a Liberal (If You Must)* (New York: Three Rivers Press, 2004), p. 149. This also appeared in Ann's syndicated column on February 14, 2002.

9. Coulter, *Godless,* p. 152. Also, a note to Ann: If you're going to insult people responsible for the education of our nation's youth, you might try to be more grammatically accurate. Your made-up word, "disinformational," is an adjectival form—which is to say, it describes the teachers, themselves, as being disinformational; it would have been better to call them "disinformation facilitators."

10. Ibid., p. 150.

11. Information taken from the Web site www.greatschools.net.

12. Information taken from the Web site www.education.net.

13. Coulter, *Godless,* p. 147.

14. Ibid., p. 158. And to be fair, Ann actually did attribute the "60 percent less" figure, citing a 2003 article called "Fringe Benefits" in *Education Next*—a group that, according to its Web site, is devoted to "bold change" in education.

15. Ibid., p. 169.

16. Ibid., p. 53.

17. Ibid., p. 150.

18. Ibid., p. 159.

19. Maureen Dowd, "Teacher Says Charter School Fired Her for Organizing to Improve Pay Scale," *New York Times,* June 28, 2006.

20. Coulter, *Godless,* p. 128.

21. Coulter, *Slander,* p. 43

22. Coulter, *Treason,* p. 287.

23. Information taken from the "My Life" biographical section of Ann's Web site, which can be found at anncoulter.org.

24. It should be noted, however, that while she attended Harvard Law for a time, Ruth Bader Ginsburg got her degree from Columbia. John Stevens, meanwhile, is the only current justice without a law degree from an Ivy League school; he got his JD from Northwestern University. The preceding information was found at the U.S. Supreme Court Web site at www.supremecourtus.gov.

25. For 2007, *U.S. News & World Report* ranks SMU's law school forty-third, tied with American University in Washington. For the *U.S. News & World Report* rankings of U.S. law schools, see www.usnews.com/usnews/edu/grad/rankings/law/brief/lawrank_brief.php.

26. Information from Ann's October 5, 2005, column, which can be found on her Web site at www.anncoulter.org.

27. Coulter, *Godless,* p. 92.

28. Ibid., p. 15.

29. Ibid.

30. Ibid., p. 5.

31. Ibid., p. 10.

32. Kanye West appeared on NBC television on September 3, 2005, as part of a telethon to raise money for victims of Hurricane Katrina.

33. Michael Shermer, *Why People Believe Weird Things—Pseudoscience, Superstition, and Other Confusions of Our Time* (New York: W. H. Freeman, 1997), p. 56.

34. "How bizarre is Ann Coulter? Deep in the weeds, let us show you," Daily Howler, April 22, 2005. http://www.dailyhowler.com/dh042205.shtml.

35. Ibid.

36. Ibid.

37. Ibid.

38. Coulter, *Slander*, p. 11.

39. Ibid.

40. Ibid., p. 12.

41. "Fighting over Florida," CBS News, November 5, 2000. The article can be found at www.cbsnews.com/stories/2000/11/05/politics/main247039.shtml.

42. Coulter, *Godless*, p. 26.

43. Christopher Reinhart, "Disparity in Death Penalty Cases and the Criminal Justice System," March 16, 2005. The study, done for the Connecticut General Assembly, can be found at www.cga.ct.gov.2005/rpt/2005-R–0215.htm.

44. Coulter, *Godless*, p. 35.

45. Steven D. Levitt and Stephen J. Dubner, *Freakonomics—A Rogue Economist Explores the Hidden Side of Everything* (New York: William Morrow, 2005), p. 121.

46. Ibid., page 122.

47. Coulter, *Godless*, p. 43.

48. Ibid.

49. Levitt and Dubner, *Freakonomics*, p. 129.

50. Ibid., p. 22.

51. Coincidentally, after Innocent III assumed the papacy in 1198, his first act was to declare a Fourth Crusade in an effort to thwart the rise of Islam. For more, see John B. Teeple, *Timelines of World History* (London: DK Publishing, 2002), p. 206.

52. Levitt and Dubner, *Freakonomics*, p. 6.

53. Coulter, *Godless*, p. 170.

54. A book detailing the incident can be found on the Cornell University Press Web site at www.cornellpress.cornell.edu.

55. Taken from Ann's Web site, www.anncoulter.org, on June 15, 2006.

56. David T. Hardy and Jason Clarke, *Michael Moore Is a Big Fat Stupid White Man* (New York: Regan Books, 2004), pp. 151–63.

57. Stephen Sherrill, "Acquired Situational Narcissism," *New York Times*, December 9, 2001.

58. Coulter, *Godless*, pp. 8–9.

59. Coulter, *Treason*, p. 250.

60. Information taken from IMDb (The Internet Movie Database) Web site, which can be found at www.imdb.com.

61. Coulter, *Treason*, p. 250.

62. Jonathan Freedland, "An Appalling Magic," *Guardian* (U.K.), May 17, 2003.

63. Coulter, *Godless*, p. 4.

64. Shermer, *Why People Believe Weird Things*, p. 55.

65. Coulter, *Slander*, p. 21.

66. Coulter, *Godless*, p. 187.

67. Coulter, *Slander*, p. 121.

68. Ibid., p. 122.

69. Ibid., p. 131.

70. Coulter, *How to Talk to a Liberal*, p. 149.

71. Coulter, *Slander*, p. 128.

72. Ibid., p. 123.

73. Ibid., p. 122.

74. Ibid., p. 127.

75. George Wayne, "She'd Rather Be Right," *Vanity Fair*, June 2006.

76. David Carr, "Deadly Intent: Ann Coulter, Word Warrior," *New York Times*, June 12, 2006.

77. Cloud, "Ms. Right," *Time*.

78. Coulter, *Slander*, p. 76.

79. Cloud, "Ms. Right," *Time*.

80. "An Appalling Magic," *Guardian.*

81. Cloud, "Ms. Right," *Time.*

82. Coulter, *How to Talk to a Liberal,* p. 18.

83. "An Appalling Magic," *Guardian.*

84. Ibid.

85. Coulter, *How to Talk to a Liberal,* p. 21.

86. Ibid, p. 400.

87. Ibid., pp. 400–4.

Chapter 3

ANN ON WOMEN

ǒʀ

MANO-A-MANO WITH THE FAIRER SEX

1. Coulter, *Slander,* p. 20.

2. Ibid., p. 75.

3. Ibid., p. 1.

4. "An Appalling Magic," *Guardian.*

5. This is from the *Cornell Review,* 1984, as reported by Cloud in "Ms. Right," *Time.*

6. While erroneously attributed on numerous Web sites as appearing in *How to Talk to a Liberal,* this quote does not appear in the text of the book but rather in promotional materials, such as those seen on the site www.conservativebookclub.com.

7. "An Appalling Magic," *Guardian.*

8. Ibid.

9. Coulter, *Slander,* pp. 42–43.

10. Fox News, *Hannity & Colmes,* May 5, 2004.

11. Kevin Leman, *The Birth Order Book—Why You Are the Way You Are* (Grand Rapids, Mich.: Revell, 1985, 1998), p. 169.

12. Ibid., pp. 173, 184.

13. Ibid., p. 188.

14. Coulter, *Slander*, p. 45.

15. Ibid., p. 46.

16. Ibid., p. 47.

17. *New York Times Book Review*, January 26, 2006.

18. Ibid.

19. Coulter, *How to Talk to a Liberal*, pp. 230–31. This also appeared in Ann's syndicated column on December 1, 2002.

20. Ibid.

21. John W. Dean, *Conservatives Without Conscience*, (New York: Viking, 2006), p. 90.

22. Elizabeth Kolbert, "Firebrand—Phyllis Schlafly and the Conservative Revolution," *The New Yorker*, November 7, 2005.

23. Coulter, *Treason*, p. 290.

24. Coulter, *Godless*, p. 8.

25. NBC, *The Tonight Show with Jay Leno*, June 14, 2006.

26. Coulter, *How to Talk to a Liberal*, p. 381. This also appeared in Ann's syndicated column in April of 1999.

27. "An Appalling Magic," *Guardian*.

28. This refers to the title of Chapter 5 in *Godless*.

29. Barbara Hagenbaugh, "Women's Pay Suffers Setback," *USA Today*, August 26, 2004.

30. Fox News, *Hannity & Colmes*, June 7, 2006. A transcript can be found at mediamatters.org.

31. Ibid.

32. Coulter, *Treason*, p. 116.

33. Coulter, *Godless*, p. 101.

34. Coulter, *Treason*, p. 290.

35. This refers to a 1997 letter to the editor that Ann Coulter wrote to the *Washington Post* in which she suggested that it was she who broke up with then boyfriend Bob Guccione Jr. and not vice versa.

36. Coulter, *How to Talk to a Liberal,* p. 8.

37. Dean, *Conservatives Without Conscience,* p. 26.

38. Ibid.

39. Coulter, *Treason,* p. 218.

40. Interestingly, when Kabuki began in Japan in the early seventeenth century, both the male and female roles were played by women. Whether Ann knows any of this or has ever actually seen Kabuki performed is a matter of speculation. As is the suggestion that she trots out a reference to it now and again simply to appear cultured.

41. From imdb.com.

42. NBC, *The Tonight Show.*

43. Ibid.

44. Coulter, *Slander,* p. 13.

Chapter 4

ANN ON SEX AND ABORTION

OR

FETUS DON'T FAIL ME NOW

1. "An Appalling Magic," *Guardian.*

2. Information taken from Media Matters for America (mediamatters. org), which describes itself as a Web-based, not-for-profit progressive research and information center dedicated to comprehensively monitoring, analyzing, and correcting conservative misinformation in the U.S. media.

3. Coulter, *How to Talk to a Liberal,* p. 171. This also appeared in Ann's syndicated column in January 2000.

4. Coulter, *Slander,* p. 3.

5. Ibid.

6. "An Appalling Magic," *Guardian.*

7. Cloud, "Ms. Right," *Time.* On a related note: Ann lives basically a few miles north of Miami, the American mecca of transvestitism. Which is not to make any allegations—those you can find on the Internet just about everywhere you look. There are, in fact, countless references to Ann's being born—or still living as—a hermaphrodite, if not simply a man in drag. As evidence, many of the sites point to her somewhat protuberant Adam's apple and a voice so huskily masculine it makes Kathleen Turner sound like Betty Boop. Whether or not they are tongue-in-(bewhiskered)-cheek, the references exist. But to be fair, evidence from her formative years, including a yearbook photo that shows her as a fair-haired athlete, indicates that Ann has always been a female.

8. *Politically Incorrect,* July 21, 1997.

9. Cloud, "Ms. Right," *Time.*

10. "'Ally McBeal' Star to Play Conservative Pundit in New TV Series," *Editor & Publisher,* July 24, 2006.

11. Coulter, *Godless,* p. 12.

12. Ibid., p. 13.

13. Ibid.

14. Jim VandeHei, "Kerry Leads in Lobby Money," *Washington Post,* January 31, 2004.

15. The photo essay on Ann can be seen at the *Time* Web site at www.time.com/time/covers/1101050425/gallery/7.html.

16. "Smart Alec," *Elle,* April 2006. The article can be found at the *Elle* Web site at www.elle.com/featurefullstory/8715/alec-baldwin.html.

17. Lloyd Grove, "Lowdown—Alec and Ann Both Vote to Abstain," New York *Daily News,* April 5, 2006.

18. Coulter, *Slander*, p. 67.

19. Coulter, *Godless*, p. 89.

20. Ibid., p. 95.

21. Kevin Freking, "Report: Women Misled on Abortion Risks," Associated Press, July 17, 2006.

22. Ibid.

23. Brendan Nyhan, "Ann Coulter: The Jargon Vanguard," Spinsanity, July 16, 2001.

24. CNBC TV, *Rivera Live*, August 2, 1999.

25. Fox News, *This Evening with Judith Regan,* August 6, 2000.

26. Coulter, *Godless*, p. 100.

27. Ibid., p. 85.

28. Ibid.

29. Ibid.

30. Ibid., p. 87.

31. Ibid., p. 91.

32. Ibid., p. 88.

33. "Smiling from the Womb," Sky News, September 12, 2003. The article can be found at www.sky.com/skynews/article/0,,300000–12773312,00.html.

34. Ellie Lee, "The Trouble with 'Smiling' Fetuses," Pro-Choice Forum, September 12, 2003. The article can be found at www.prochoiceforum. org.uk/ocr_ethical_iss1.asp.

35. Coulter, *Godless*, p. 192.

36. "House Sustains Bush's Veto of Stem Cell Bill," Fox News, July 20, 2006.

37. Coulter, *Godless*, p. 193.

38. "House Sustains Bush's Veto of Stem Cell Bill," Fox News.

39. Coulter, *Godless*, pp. 192–93.

40. Ibid., p. 195.

41. Sam Harris, *The End of Faith—Religion, Terror, and the Future of Reason* (New York: W. W. Norton, 2004), p. 165.

42. Coulter, *Godless*, pp. 102–3.

43. Harris, *The End of Faith*, p. 109.

44. Ibid., pp. 192–93.

45. Ibid., pp. 166–67.

46. Coulter, *Godless*, p. 195.

47. Jackie Calmes, "Stem-Cell Issue: Republicans' Undoing?," *Wall Street Journal*, July 21, 2006.

48. Coulter, *Godless*, p. 195.

49. A number of sources indicate that the name Godiva is the Latinate version of the Anglo-Saxon for "gift of God," which seems appropriate given Ann Coulter's self-appointed status as the religious right's leading light.

Chapter 5

ANN ON RELIGION

OR

THERE'S ONLY "RIGHT" AND WRONG

1. "An Appalling Magic," *Guardian*.

2. This refers to Ann's suggestion that we deal with homosexuality as per Muslim Sharia law by dropping a wall on anyone found "guilty" of it, as detailed in the chapter "Ann Has It Both Ways."

3. Coulter, *Godless*, p. 269.

4. Harris, *The End of Faith*, pp. 171–72. It should be noted, however, that Harris later argues against moral relativism and the related notion of pragmatism. Still, his point is that the Good Book should not be confused with a guidebook.

5. Coulter, *Godless*, p. 2.

6. Ibid., p. 3.

7. Coulter, *Treason*, p. 1.

8. Jean-Jacques Rousseau, *The Social Contract* (New York: Barnes & Noble, 2005), p. xv.

9. Ibid., p. xiv.

10. Ibid.

11. Daniel C. Dennet, *Darwin's Dangerous Idea—Evolution and the Meanings of Life* (New York: Simon & Schuster, 1995), p. 17.

12. Ibid., p. 18.

13. Ibid., p. 22.

14. Coulter, *Godless*, p. 12.

15. "An Appalling Magic," *Guardian*.

16. Coulter, *Slander*, p. 211.

17. Coulter, *How to Talk to a Liberal*, p. 124. This also appeared in Ann's syndicated column on January 7, 2004.

18. Said to Pat Robertson on *The 700 Club* on October 2, 2002, as transcribed by the American Politics Journal, which can be found at http://www.americanpolitics.com/20020205Coulter.html.

19. Coulter, *Godless*, p. 2.

20. Cambridge, Massachusetts. City ordinances can be found on the city's Web site, at http://bpc.iserver.net/codes/cbridge/index.htm

21. Cloud, "Ms. Right," *Time*.

22. Ibid.

23. Coulter, *Godless*, p. 281.

Chapter 6

ANN HAS IT BOTH WAYS
ᴏʀ
MIGHTY (HERM)APHRODITE

1. Coulter, *Godless*, p. 67.

2. Ibid., p. 26.

3. Ibid., p. 59.

4. Coulter, *Treason,* p. 75.

5. Ibid., p. 66.

6. Cloud, "Ms. Right," *Time.*

7. Ibid.

8. Coulter, *Treason,* pp. 69–70, 76, 101.

9. Ibid., p. 194.

10. Coulter, *Godless,* p. 92.

11. Linda Greenhouse, *Becoming Justice Blackmun* (New York: Henry Holt, 2005), p. 214.

12. Coulter, *Godless,* p. 106.

13. Julian Baggini and Peter S. Fosl, *The Philosopher's Toolkit* (Malden, Mass.: Blackwell, 2003), p. 12.

14. Coulter, *Godless,* p. 167.

15. Charol Shakeshaft, "Educator Sexual Misconduct: A Synthesis of Existing Literature," 2004. The study can be found at the Department of Education Web site, www.ed.gov.rschstat/research/pubs/misconductreview/report.pdf.

16. The information was taken from the Hofstra University Web site at www.hofstra.edu/News/Ur/PressRoom/presroom_shakeshaft.cfm.

17. Coulter, *Slander,* p. 214.

18. Coulter, *Treason,* p. 215. This also appeared in Ann's syndicated column on July 12, 2006.

19. KOA Radio, *The John Caldara Show,* July 12, 2006. A transcript of Ann's appearance on the show can be found at the Media Matters for America Web site at www.mediamatters.org/items/200607140015.

20. Jacob Bernstein "Memo Pad: Fan Mail," *Women's Wear Daily,* July 18, 2006. The article can be found at www.wwd.com/issue/article/107729.

21. KOA Radio, *The John Caldara Show.*

22. Ibid.

23. Ibid.

Chapter 7

ANN ON 9/11

☞

WITH FRIENDS LIKE ANN, WHO NEEDS ENEMIES?

1. Coulter, *Treason*, p. 26. This also appeared in Ann's syndicated column on September 12, 2001.

2. Coulter, "It's 'Let's Roll,' Not 'Let's Roll Over,'" August 11, 2005.

3. Coulter, *Godless*, p. 103.

4. Ibid.

5. "NBC News Slanders Ann Coulter," *NewsMax*, July 2006.

6. Bill Carter, "MSNBC's Star Carves Anti-Fox Niche," the *New York Times*, July 11, 2006.

7. NBC, *The Tonight Show*.

8. Coulter, *How to Talk to a Liberal*, p. 12.

9. A transcript of the May 22, 2006, broadcast of *The Radio Factor* can be found at Media Matters at www. mediamatters.org/items/200605240012.

10. Ibid.

11. Fox News, *The O'Reilly Factor*, August 5, 2005. A transcript of the broadcast can be found at www.foxnews.com/story.0,2933,164866,00.html.

12. Cloud, "Ms. Right," *Time*.

13. Fox News, *The O'Reilly Factor*, June 7, 2006. A transcript can be found at Media Matters at www.mediamatters.org/items/200606090001.

14. MSNBC, *Hardball with Chris Matthews*, July 14, 2006. A transcript can be found at www.mediamatters.org/items/2006071500002.

15. Mike Straka, "Grrr!," foxnews.com, June 8, 2006.

16. NBC, *The Tonight Show*.

17. Straka, "Grrr!," foxnews.com.

18. Coulter, *Godless*, p. 105.

19. Ibid.

20. Ibid., p. 108.

21. Ibid., p. 109.

22. Ibid.

23. Ibid.

24. Shermer, *Why People Believe Weird Things*, p. 57.

25. Coulter, *Godless*, p. 109.

26. "Sept. 11 Attacks Timeline," *USA Today*, June 16, 2004.

27. Ann provided a photo of the Coulter children as part of the aforementioned photo essay on the *Time* magazine Web site. In the snapshot, dated 1965, Ann is shown standing in front of her two brothers. And she ain't two years old, that's for sure. Bottom line: The smart money says Ann is older than she sometimes admits to being. The photo of Ann and her brothers can be seen at www.time.com/time/covers/1101050425/gallery/7.html.

28. Coulter, *Godless*, pp. 112–13.

29. Ibid., p. 113.

30. Coulter, *Treason*, p. 76.

31. Ibid., p. 2.

32. Ibid., p. 253.

33. Associated Press, December 21, 2002.

34. Ibid.

35. Coulter, *Treason*, p. 248.

36. Ibid., pp. 248–49.

37. Ibid., p. 214.

38. Coulter, *Godless*, p. 6.

39. Coulter, *How to Talk to a Liberal,* p. 12.

40. Coulter, *Treason,* p. 130.

41. Ibid., p. 75.

42. Statistics on Americans' shifting support for the Vietnam War can be found at www.seanet.com/~jimxc/Politics/Mistakes/Vietnam_support. html.

43. Coulter, *How to Talk to a Liberal,* p. 58. This also appeared in Ann's syndicated column on March 28, 2003.

44. "Forces: U.S. & Coalition/Casualties," CNN.com. The report can be found at www.cnn.com/SPECIALS/2003/iraq/forces/casualties/.

45. Ibid., p. 74. This also appeared in Ann's syndicated column on November 5, 2003.

46. Ibid., p. 83. Also Ann's column on June 3, 2004.

47. Ibid., p. 58. Also Ann's column on March 28, 2003.

48. Teeple, *Timelines of World History,* p. 434.

49. This quote is taken from the Ann Coulter Doll available for order from a Web site called TalkingPresidents.com.

Chapter 8

ANN AND RESEARCH
ᴏ̅ʀ̅
WHEN THE CAT'S AWAY, THE MICE WILL PLAGIARIZE

1. Information taken from gawker.com, June 13, 2006.

2. Coulter, *How to Talk to a Liberal,* p. 21.

3. From gawker.com, June 13, 2006.

4. Information taken from The Rude Pundit, June 9, 2006.

5. Ibid.

6. Ibid.

7. Ibid.

8. Philip Recchia, "Copycatty Coulter Pilfers Prose: Pro," *New York Post*, July 2, 2006.

9. Information taken from NewsMax.com.

10. Al Franken, *Lies and the Lying Liars Who Tell Them—A Fair and Balanced Look at the Right* (New York: Dutton, 2003), p. 12.

11. "Who, outside of New York City, reads the *New York Times*?" Ann asks on page 42 of *Slander*. Answer: With just over half of the newspaper's paid weekday circulation of more than a million copies being sold outside the New York metropolitan area, a boatload of people do. And, apparently, she's one of 'em, despite living in Palm Beach.

12. Coulter, *Godless*, p. 208.

13. Shermer, *Why People Believe Weird Things*, p. 57.

14. Coulter, *Treason*, p. 185.

15. Ibid., pp. 9, 40, 138–39, 142, 144–45, 154, 158–59, 163–64, 171, 173, 175, 184, 186, 190, 199. (Oh, come on—you didn't expect me to cite all those individually, did you?)

16. Ibid., p. 96.

17. Coulter, *Godless*, p. 298.

18. "An Appalling Magic," *Guardian*.

19. NBC, *The Tonight Show*.

20. CNN, *The Situation Room*, July 7, 2006, report by Brian Todd.

21. Dean, *Conservatives Without Conscience*, p. 24.

Chapter 9

ANN SPEAKS
ᴏ̃ʀ̃
UNDER A SERIES OF MEN IS NOT THE ONLY PLACE SHE LIES

1. Coulter, *Godless*, p. 99.

2. *Webster's Encyclopedic Unabridged Dictionary of the English Language* (New York: Gramercy Books, 1994), p. 1212.

3. Coulter, *Godless*, p. 206.

4. David Hume, *An Enquiry Concerning Human Understanding* (New York: Barnes & Noble, 2004), p. 95.

5. Coulter *Slander*, p. 199.

6. Ibid.

7. Shermer, *Why People Believe Weird Things*, p. 49.

8. Ibid., p. 51.

9. Coulter, *Godless*, p. 201.

10. *Webster's*, p. 1471.

11. Ibid.

12. Coulter, *Godless*, p. 152.

13. Ibid., p. 203.

14. Humphrey Bogart's character in the movie *Casablanca* never actually utters the phrase "Play it again, Sam." Early in the movie, Ilsa, played by Ingrid Bergman, says, "Play it, Sam. Play 'As Time Goes By.'" Bogart's Rick later tells the piano player, "You played it for her, you can play it for me!" and then, "If she can stand it, I can! Play it!" Memorable quotes from the movie can be found at imdb.com.

15. Coulter, *Godless*, p. 207.

16. Ibid., p. 208.

17. Shermer, *Why People Believe Weird Things*, p. 52.

18. Ibid., p. 58.

19. Coulter, *Godless*, p. 212.

20. Brian Krebs, "12 Microsoft Patches Plug 21 Security Holes," *Washington Post*, June 13, 2006.

21. David Quammen, "Was Darwin Wrong?" *National Geographic*, November 2004.

22. Coulter, *Godless*, p. 211.

23. Tim M. Berra, *Evolution and the Myth of Creationism* (Stanford, Calif.: Stanford University Press, 1990), p. 41.

24. Coulter, *Godless*, p. 211.

25. Berra, *Evolution and the Myth of Creationism*, p. 40.

26. Coulter, *Godless*, p. 218.

27. Ibid., p. 219.

28. Ibid., p. 225.

29. For more on this, see Shermer, *Why People Believe Weird Things*, p. 55.

30. "While Most Americans Believe in God, Only 36% Attend a Religious Service Once a Month or More Often," Harris Poll, October 15, 2003. Results can be seen at www.harrisinteractive.com/harris_poll/index.asp?PID=408.

31. Nyhan, "Ann Coulter: The Jargon Vanguard," Spinsanity.

32. Coulter, *Godless*, p. 25.

33. Ibid.

34. Ibid., pp. 5–6.

35. Ibid., p. 6.

36. Ibid.

37. Coulter, *Slander*, p. 116.

38. Ibid.

39. Ibid., p. 73.

40. Ibid.

41. Ibid., p. 38.

42. Franken, *Lies and the Lying Liars Who Tell Them*, p. 6.

43. Coulter, *Slander*, p. 261.

44. Robert Lipsyte, "Stock Car Star Killed on Last Lap of Daytona 500," *New York Times*, February 19, 2001.

45. Cloud, "Ms. Right," *Time*.

46. Ibid.